"I'm grateful to be Jarvis Masters's teacher in part because he has taught me so much. I have rarely encountered anyone who expresses the essence of Buddhism in a clearer, more moving way than he does, and I deeply admire how David Sheff has captured that hard-won wisdom in this book."

—PEMA CHÖDRÖN, Buddhist teacher and author of
When Things Fall Apart

"This is a beautiful, profoundly spiritual book, and a page turner. Jarvis Jay Masters' transformation from an unloved child of violence and poverty to Buddhist teacher on Death Row, is thrilling. Reading it changed me, threw the lights on, opened and gentled my heart. I'm going to give it to everyone I know."

—ANNE LAMOTT

"An inspiring book about how meaning can be found even in—perhaps especially in—adversity. It's a study of Buddhism, of criminal justice, of the ways people connect with each other, and it's written with deep feeling and verve."

—ANDREW SOLOMON

David Sheff is the author of many books, including the #1 *New York Times* bestselling memoir *Beautiful Boy*, which was turned into a movie starring Steve Carell and Timothée Chalamet. His work has appeared in *Outside, Rolling Stone, Wired, Fortune* and elsewhere. His piece for *The New York Times*, 'My Addicted Son' received an award from the American Psychological Association for Outstanding Contribution to Advancing the Understanding of Addictions.

DAVID SHEFF

THE BUDDHIST ON DEATH ROW

ONE PLACE. MANY STORIES

AUTHOR'S NOTE:
Some of the names and details in this book have been changed at the request of
participants concerned about their privacy or, in some cases, their safety.

HQ
An imprint of HarperCollins*Publishers* Ltd
1 London Bridge Street
London SE1 9GF

www.harpercollins.co.uk

HarperCollins*Publishers*
1st Floor, Watermarque Building, Ringsend Road
Dublin 4, Ireland

This edition 2022

I

First published in Great Britain by .
HQ, an imprint of HarperCollins*Publishers* Ltd 2020
Published in the United States by Simon & Schuster,
1230 Avenue of the Americas
New York, NY 10020

ISBN: 978-0-00-839547-6

Printed and Bound in the UK using 100% Renewable Electricity
at CPI Group (UK) Ltd

MIX
Paper from
responsible sources
FSC
www.fsc.org   FSC™ C007454

This book is produced from independently certified FSC™ paper
to ensure responsible forest management.

For more information visit: www.harpercollins.co.uk/green

For Pamela Krasney, who inspired us with her moral courage as she fought for criminal justice reform and an end to the death penalty. Pamela made the world a better place for her family, friends, and countless others.

Cage an eagle and it will bite at the
wires, be they of iron or of gold.

—HENRIK IBSEN

CONTENTS

CONTENTS

INTRODUCTION

I sit in a molded plastic chair on one side of a small table opposite a man named Jarvis Jay Masters. I tell him I'm considering writing a book about him and ask what he thinks of the idea. I emphasize that if I go forward, I'll report what I find, both the good and the bad.

"I can't be painted worse than I've been painted," Masters says, and I guess that's true for someone convicted of murder.

"I mean," he adds, "look where we are."

Where we are is in a closet-sized cage among a dozen similar cages in a visitation hall reserved for the condemned at San Quentin State Prison.

I follow Masters's gaze as it sweeps the other cages in which convicted killers sit with family members or attorneys. Ramón

Bojórquez Salcido, convicted of murdering seven people, including his wife and daughters, sits with his lawyer in a cage opposite ours. Nearby, Richard Allen Davis, who raped and killed a twelve-year-old girl, munches Doritos. In the cage on the end, near a bookshelf lined with board games and Bibles, Scott Peterson, convicted of murdering his eight-months-pregnant wife and their unborn child, sits with his sister.

Peterson looks relaxed and fit, but some prisoners appear tense, agitated, or sullen. And then there are guys—diminutive, bespectacled, innocuous—who look like tellers or, in one case, John Oliver. Their looks deceive, Masters says. Over the years, he's been surprised when he's learned about the crimes committed by the meekest and politest of his death row neighbors. "Some of them have perfect manners, place their napkins on their laps, but half of Iowa is missing."

In 2006, my friend Pamela Krasney, an activist devoted to prison reform and other social justice causes, told me about a death row inmate who, she claimed, had been wrongly convicted of murder. He was unlike anyone she'd ever known—more conscious, wise, and empathetic "in spite of his past." She corrected herself. "*Because* of his past."

Introduced by Masters's friend, the famed Buddhist nun Pema Chödrön, Pamela had been visiting Masters regularly for years. She belonged to a group of supporters devoted to proving his innocence. They called themselves Jarvistas.

Pamela told me that Masters had written a book, numerous articles, and a poem for which he'd won a PEN award. He'd converted to Buddhism and studied with an eminent Tibetan lama, Chagdud Tulku Rinpoche, who proclaimed him a bodhisattva, "one who works to end suffering in a place drowning in suffering." Indeed, Pamela claimed that Masters had become a force for good in San Quentin, teaching Buddhism to inmates and even thwarting violence.

Encouraged by Pamela, I arranged a visit to death row, arriving at the former Bay of Skulls on a fogless morning, a steel wind blowing in through the Golden Gate. White sailboats floated like lotus petals on the bay. Tugboats pushed barges, hydrofoil ferries glided by, and the Richmond–San Rafael Bridge glistened. After my identity was verified, I passed through a metal detector and, as instructed, followed a painted yellow line along a rocky embankment. Overhead, armed guards watched from a tower that looked like a lighthouse.

Masters was housed in the ominously named Adjustment Center, the solitary-housing unit—"the hole"—once described by a San Quentin administrator as a "contained, enclosed unit for the vicious, violent, insane—men society doesn't want to exist." He'd been in the AC for two decades.

I was led to a chair that faced a smeared glass partition. After several minutes, a door opened on the other side, and a guard escorted Masters in. He was tall and clean shaven, with neatly buzzed hair. Reading glasses hung around his neck.

When he was unshackled, Masters sat, and we picked up cracked handsets. His voice was muffled, as if we were talking through tin-can telephones.

Masters had clear brown eyes, a sweet tenor voice, and a quiet charisma that the glass couldn't obstruct. We talked about Pamela, Pema, writing, the news, and a recent lockdown after a stabbing. I asked questions about guards, inmates, and his Buddhist practice. Masters was articulate, thoughtful, and funny. After an hour and a half, a guard signaled that the visit was over. He led Masters away, and I left the cellblock, emerging into the cold bay air.

I ruminated about the meeting. Masters seemed open and earnest. I glimpsed what his friends described as something indefinably special about him, but charm does not equal innocence. We've read about vicious yet charismatic murderer: Truman Capote's Perry Smith (Capote even grew fond of his accomplice, the far more pitiless Richard Hickock), Sister Helen Prejean's Elmo Patrick Sonnier and Robert Lee Willie, and Norman Mailer's Gary Gilmore (as Mailer portrayed him, Gilmore was callous and remorseless but had a keen mind, wit, and allure).

Was Masters a killer? His friends swore that he wasn't. Had he been framed, as his lawyers argued? Or was he a skilled manipulator, a con artist taking advantage of trusting, good-hearted people like Pamela and Pema?

Even if Masters was innocent, I didn't know what to think about the claims that he was, as his supporters described him, an enlightened Buddhist practitioner who had changed and saved lives. There are Buddhists in many prisons. For that matter, there are born-again inmates of every faith. There are prison writers, poets, and others who've been singled out as unique. Was Masters truly different? I refrained from judging him either kindly or harshly. But he continued to intrigue me.

In the years that followed, Pamela kept me abreast of events in Masters's life. In 2007, after twenty-two years, he was released from solitary confinement and moved to a less restrictive death row cellblock. The following year he married in a ceremony presided over by Pema Chödrön. In 2009, Pamela asked me to provide a blurb for the second book Masters wrote. She also told me about the ongoing appeals process. There was no question in her mind that he'd be exonerated; it was only a matter of time.

Then, in 2015, Pamela died of a rare blood disease. Pema conducted a Buddhist funeral, during which she read a letter from Jarvis. The memorial was held in Mill Valley, California, across the county from San Quentin. As Pema read Masters's eulogy, I thought of him in his death row cell a few miles away. I also thought of Pamela's deep connection with and devotion to Jarvis and recalled her claims that he inspired and helped countless people inside San Quentin and beyond its walls. Soon after I left the memorial, I decided to investigate her claims.

I spoke to people in San Quentin and some on the outside. Pema told me she'd read Masters's book, wrote to him, and then visited. They developed a close friendship. She admired his ability to bear weight that would crush most people and the joy he exuded in a joyless place. His interpretations of Buddhist teachings inspired her, and his insights helped her achieve a deeper understanding of Buddhist concepts she thought she knew.

I read letters from others who'd also read his books and were inspired to write him about hardships they faced: abusive relationships, losses of loved ones, illness, and depression. Several wrote about suicide attempts. Masters responded to all those letters, and their authors wrote back to thank him for the solace, guidance, and hope he'd given them.

There were letters from "troubled" teenagers who had been given his book by counselors or teachers. High school teachers who had assigned Masters's book in their classes sent packets of letters from students he'd inspired. A librarian in Watts said that his book was stolen more than any other on her shelves.

More remarkably, I was able to confirm that Masters had defended prisoners who were vulnerable to attack because they were gay, were suspected of informing on other inmates, or had otherwise run afoul of prison's cruel norms. Even more extraordinary, he averted potential attacks by prisoners on correctional officers (COs). I spoke to people, including a guard, who said Masters had prevented their suicides. The CO told me that his young son was gravely ill, that he and his wife were fighting constantly, he was drinking heavily, and he loathed his job. The guard admitted he treated inmates like scum, which was how he viewed them. He confessed he had planned to kill himself.

One early morning, Masters called out to the officer, who was walking the tier. Jarvis said he'd noticed that the man seemed stressed and down and wanted to make sure he was doing all right. The guard wasn't one to open up about his personal life to anyone, least of all a con, but "something about Masters" caused him to confide in him about his son and problems at home. The conversation led to months of predawn talks at Masters's cell door, during which Jarvis helped the guard face his son's illness, support his wife, and enter a program to stop drinking. The officer no longer thought about taking his own life; instead, he embraced the life he had.

The CO said that his job became meaningful when Masters helped him realize he could help people who desperately needed it; he no longer saw it as herding cattle but as an opportunity to treat the suffering with compassion. His attitude transformed because "Masters showed me that most of the cons just were dealt a raw hand. They're just people, some more fucked-up than others, some no more fucked-up than people on the outside. They all had miserable lives—and they all have souls."

These and similar stories convinced me to go forward with this book.

In the four years since then, I've made more than 150 trips to death row and recorded more than 100 hours of conversation. I've also spoken with Masters for untold hours by phone. I supplemented our conversations with his writings—his books, letters, journals, and short stories—but I mostly relied on Masters's own memories and prison stories. He spoke candidly, but he was cautious when it came to guards, and he was protective of other inmates. However, he was unsparingly candid about his own life. He spoke extensively about the violence in his past, and he teared up when he talked about his victims.

I struggled to determine if I could rely on Masters's recollections of events, including some that had taken place more than fifty years ago. Many of the people described in this book are dead or locked away and unable or unwilling to talk to me. (Some couldn't be dissuaded of their belief that I was police.) Unsurprisingly, few guards and inmates agreed to talk, and of those who did, most spoke under the condition that they wouldn't be identifiable. In the end, I found that Masters's stories that could be independently verified proved to be accurate.

Over our hundreds of hours together, Jarvis and I talked about many subjects, but most of our conversations wended, by way of curves, spirals, and trapdoors, to questions of being: if and how people can change their nature and how we can find relief from pain and meaning in our lives.

As I pieced together Masters's journey, I saw how he found the answers to these questions through meditation and Buddhism.

I'm not a Buddhist, but as I learned how his faith helped him, I discovered how its tenets and practices can help others—believers and nonbelievers alike. I learned that people *can* change and how but also that transformation comes in fits and starts. The journey forward isn't linear but cyclical, and it's hard. I learned something else that was even more profound: that the process and goal are different from what many of us expect. Instead of working to change our true nature, we must find it. Instead of running from suffering, we must embrace it.

Masters never claimed to have seen a light or been born again. He dismisses those who speak of him as a teacher. He cringed when I told him that people described him as enlightened. "I don't even know what that word means," he objected, and he emphasized that he's "the last person" who should be considered a spokesperson for Buddhism, admitting that his form of the faith is ramshackle and geared toward the particular challenges presented by life on death row. However, as Masters surmounted internal and external obstacles, he gained insights into issues many of us struggle with, and over time I learned why people said he inspired them.

Set in a place of unremitting violence, insanity, confusion, and rage, Masters's story traverses the haunted caverns and tributaries of loneliness, despair, trauma, and other suffering—terrain we all know too well—and arrives at healing, meaning, and wisdom. Again and again, I have felt deeply Masters's power to inspire, and I hope I can share some of that power in the pages that follow.

PART ONE

THE FIRST NOBLE TRUTH

SUFFERING

Hurt people hurt people.

— "Warlock," former Crips shot-caller,
in a GRIP (Guiding Rage into Power)
class at San Quentin State Prison

1

BORN USELESS

In the spring of 1986, Melody Ermachild ventured inside the imposing brick-and-stone edifice of San Quentin State Prison to meet her new client, Jarvis Jay Masters, a twenty-four-year-old African American kid from Harbor City, California. Masters had arrived at San Quentin five years earlier after being convicted of thirteen counts of armed robbery and sentenced to twenty years in prison. He'd subsequently been charged with conspiring to kill a prison guard and making the knife used in the murder. He had been moved to the Adjustment Center—solitary confinement—and was now on trial. If he was found guilty, he could be put to death.

Masters wore a navy blue knit cap pulled down to his eyes. He leaned back in his chair, arms folded across his chest, and barely acknowledged her. She explained that she was a criminal investigator hired by his legal team to write a social history of his life. If he was convicted, they hoped her report would help his lawyers convince the judge and jury that he should be spared the death penalty. To prepare the report, she would need to interview him, his family, his foster parents, and others who'd known him.

When she mentioned his family, Masters broke his silence. "Keep them out of it," he growled. His eyes, cold and blank until then, were blazing. "They have nothing to say about me."

He said no more during that meeting, and he kept his sullen silence throughout a dozen more visits during which Melody reviewed the case against him and tried to get him to open up.

One morning, Melody showed up in the visiting booth on crutches. She'd been rock climbing and had fallen, rupturing her Achilles tendon.

As usual, she pulled out files and notebooks. Also as usual, Masters regarded her with disdainful silence.

Suddenly Melody snapped, "Do you think this is a joke?"

He was startled.

"They want to *kill* you!" she said, her voice rising.

She had never blown up at a client before, and she immediately apologized.

"It's not just my leg," she explained. In her distress, she set aside her usual professional demeanor and poured out the reasons for her despondency. "I had a baby when I was a teenager, and I was forced to put him up for adoption," she said. "I never got over it. After twenty years, I just heard from my son and we met."

Jarvis stared.

"It was wonderful meeting him, just what I'd always wanted, but it stirred up a lot. I've been spending a lot of time crying."

After a pause, she added, "I've been thinking a lot about my childhood. My father died when I was little. My mother was depressed, and she would"—Melody stopped and inhaled—"she would beat us. Later I got pregnant, and they threw me out. I found a home for pregnant girls, where the baby was born. I thought about killing myself. Many times."

Jarvis spoke for the first time. "That is some fucked-up shit."

His perfect summation made her smile.

Their eyes met briefly; then he looked away.

Jarvis was less hostile after that. Sometimes he arrived in the visiting room as taciturn as ever, but other times he was less guarded. He began to consider her questions seriously and answer them honestly. They talked about the case and his past, though the conversations sometimes stirred up painful memories and he would shut down. Ultimately, though, he agreed to let her interview his family.

Melody flew to Los Angeles to meet his mother, Cynthia Campbell, whom Jarvis hadn't seen for seven years, since the day of his arrest that landed him in San Quentin in 1981. After he was implicated in a string of armed robberies, police issued an APB for him, and Jarvis hid out at one friend's house after another, no place more than a couple of nights. One afternoon he was at his sister's apartment. A police scanner was on, and he heard them coming. But there wasn't time to run. A voice from a bullhorn told him to come outside with his hands up.

An officer pinned Jarvis down on the hood of a squad car and cuffed his hands behind his back. Cynthia, who'd been staying downstairs at the apartment of Jarvis's other sister, ran outside. Sobbing and screaming, she attacked an officer, punching and clawing him. Jarvis watched the police wrestle her to the ground.

When Melody met Cynthia in her shabby living room, she seemed frail and sad. There were remnants of beauty in her face but it showed the pall of decades of addiction. Cynthia's honesty surprised Melody. In a raspy smoker's voice, she said she'd become a mother at sixteen. She'd had eight children in all. She admitted, "I left Jarvis feeling like he was a motherless child, but I couldn't do any better."

Before she left, Melody asked Cynthia if she'd consider visiting Jarvis—"I think it would do him good"—and Cynthia agreed to come.

Back in the prison, Jarvis wanted to hear every detail about the visit. As Melody talked, he pictured his mother. He remembered her beauty and gentleness but also her absence and volatility. He recalled sitting with her watching TV, and then she would get up and disappear. After a while he'd go look for her and find her passed out on the toilet in a heroin stupor. He would try to wake her up and get her to bed. Every time, he was afraid she might be dead.

He also remembered the men who came and went. He ran into a stranger in the living room, and Cynthia would say, "Give Jarvis some money, Daddy." Then to Jarvis, "Run down and get some candy."

Though he'd been only five, Jarvis vividly recalled the day police came to the house and found him and his sisters living in squalor. Social workers took the children to Child Protective Services, where they were separated. Jarvis was taken to a small room with two gentle-seeming women. One lifted him onto a table and removed his shirt. They looked in horror at the bruises and scars that covered his body.

Jarvis shook that memory aside and instead looked ahead to his mother's visit. He thought of the things he wanted to tell her most: he missed her, and he loved her.

Jarvis put his mother's name on his visitors list, and he eagerly awaited her arrival. But she never showed up. One morning, through the bars of his cell door, he saw the prison chaplain approaching. Inmates knew that the chaplain didn't come around just to chat. His visit meant bad news.

The chaplain told Jarvis that one of his sisters had called with a message. Their mother had a heart attack. She didn't make it.

The chaplain said, "I'm sorry, Masters," and left the tier.

Jarvis began trembling, and then his shock morphed into fury. He pounded his fists into the cell wall until his knuckles bled.

For weeks, he remained distraught over his mother's death and fuming because he wasn't allowed to attend her funeral. He paced his cell, refused yard time, and cursed out a guard who, in response, slammed him into a wall.

Meanwhile, Melody continued to interview people for her report, and she was delighted when she could bring news that might pick up Jarvis's spirits. She'd been in touch with his younger sister, Carlette, who planned to come up from Los Angeles to see him.

Jarvis added another name to his list of approved visitors, and this time it was not in vain. On the morning of the visit, he was escorted to the visiting hall where his sister waited on the other side of a Plexiglas window.

Carlette began crying when she saw him. Finally she collected herself enough to speak his name: "Jarvis." She stared at her big brother and said it again: "Jarvis."

Jarvis responded without emotion. He gave a slight nod before asking, "What's up, baby sister?"

She asked, "Are you all right?"

"I'm fine," he said flatly.

"What's it been like in there? Are you okay?"

He shrugged. "What do you think?"

She repeated, *"Are you okay?"*

"Yeah," he said. "No big deal. Motherfuckers fighting, stabbing."

She looked alarmed.

"Don't worry about me, little sister," he said. "No one will fuck with me."

Carlette noticed faded tattoos on her brother's temple and wrist, the number 255, and asked about them.

When they were children, they lived on 255th Street in Harbor City.

"What made you get that?" she asked.

"It was something I'd seen on a homeboy lying in a coffin."

Carlette was aghast.

When a guard came by with a five-minute warning, Jarvis asked Carlette if she could put money in his trust account so he could buy cigarettes.

She said okay, and she left.

It was an expensive ordeal for Carlette to travel by car from LA, but she returned a month later, this time with her young son, who sat on her lap. Once again, Jarvis regaled her with prison stories. It saddened her that he acted as though prison were a joke, and she was disgusted when he boasted that he was feared and envied as a "warrior" in some revolution.

The third time Carlette came, Jarvis started up again, talking about the race war in San Quentin—in which black inmates were defending themselves against attacks by Mexican and white gangs—about crooked guards selling drugs and guns, and about a stabbing, as if these horrifying events were amusing.

Carlette burst into tears.

Jarvis stared. "What are you crying about?"

She blurted out, "What about *us*?"

He didn't understand.

"You're always telling me about your life like you're a hard gangster, some revolutionary, all that bullshit. You never ask about us. Why should I even come see you? What about me? What about your nephew? You know what he said after last time we saw you? 'Mama, I wanna be just like Uncle Jay.' What am I supposed to tell him?"

She cried harder, but Jarvis just rolled his eyes.

She continued, "You think when your homeboys get out they're going to send you money? You think they're going to write you, send pictures of their children? Do you even *think* about us? Who are you trying to impress? *What is wrong with you?*"

Still sobbing, she picked up her son and left.

Jarvis sat fuming. What was wrong with *him*? What the fuck was wrong with *her*? She had no idea who he was. She had no idea *where* he was. His sister was a fool, and he didn't care if she never came back.

In his cell that night, Jarvis tried to put the visit out of his mind, but he kept thinking about something Carlette had said. Many of the men he knew in prison were in for life, but some would get out eventually. Would he hear from them? Would they write? Would they send money or pictures of their children? Would they visit?

Not a chance.

What *had* he been trying to prove? Who was he trying to impress?

Even harder to ignore was her other question: "What is wrong with you?"

He tried to blow it off, but he couldn't. He huddled in a corner of his cell. He felt . . . he didn't know what. Something he didn't want to feel.

Jarvis had often contemplated death, having seen it from a very young age. He'd imagined being shot like many of the boys he knew in his neighborhood. Other times, he saw himself going out in a blaze of gunfire like in a movie. Sometimes he even looked forward to death. It would be a relief.

Throughout that long night, he confronted a thought he'd never let himself think before: He wanted to get out of prison, to reconnect with his family, to be his sister's big brother and his nephew's uncle. He wanted to *live*.

Using the only writing implement he was allowed—the insert of a ballpoint pen (a pen could be a weapon)—he placed a sheet of paper on his bunk, using it as a desk, and wrote to Carlette. He thanked her for her help, her letters, her visits. He wrote that he was proud of the woman she'd become and her beautiful son, and he apologized for never asking about her life; he wanted to know everything about it.

He feared that he'd never see her again. And he still couldn't get her question out of his head: *What is wrong with me?*

*　　*　　*

Jarvis was nineteen when he arrived at San Quentin. When he went out to the yard for the first time, he saw men playing basketball on courts with sagging, netless rims. Other cons lifted weights, sat across from one another on benches and played checkers or cards, or clustered in groups talking. Races did not mingle.

When a stranger approached, Jarvis was wary until the man dropped the name of Halifu, an inmate he'd met at Los Angeles County Jail. Halifu was physically imposing but spoke like a professor. He was some kind of revolutionary. He bent Jarvis's ear, talking about the historical oppression of African Americans, quoting W. E. B. Du Bois, Marcus Garvey, Angela Davis, and Malcolm X and educating Jarvis about the Black Panthers and an "organization" called the Black Guerrilla Family. Halifu said the BGF, cofounded by W. L. Nolen and George Jackson, had been created in response to a spate of killings of African American inmates in US prisons. He said that Jarvis needed to join the revolution and began calling him Askari, the Swahili word for "soldier."

Later, when Halifu learned that Jarvis was heading to San Quentin, he sent word to "comrades" there, including the man who approached him on the yard. The prisoner, whose Swahili name was Fuma, had been in the San Quentin contingent of the Black Panther Party when Jackson was killed in the prison in 1971. Fuma introduced Jarvis to other "revolutionaries," including teachers responsible for educating "kezi," the men who aspired to join the BGF. A blackboard was set up on the yard and classes of sixty or so kezi gathered for instructions. Those who'd never gone to school were taught to read and write, and all of them learned about black nationalism and the class struggle.

That political education justified and focused Jarvis's rage. Angry and alienated, he was primed for radicalization—and to connect to something bigger than himself. In the name Black Guerrilla Family, "family" was the operative word for young men like Jarvis, as its members embraced them like fathers and brothers.

Jarvis and the other kezi knew that only a handful of them would be accepted into the BGF. They were told, "Many are called but few are chosen." Jarvis was determined to be one of the chosen few. He trained with diligence and commitment, and, as a former BGF member recounted, Jarvis was among a handful of dedicated soldiers who made the cut. They were initiated in a solemn ceremony at which they were given pins with the five-pointed red Communist star to wear on their lapels. Then they were awarded "fraternal membership" in the gang. A commander said, "There are new dragons among us. They have risen into the ranks of jamaa (family)."

Two years later, in 1985, a BGF member broke from the organization's leadership and planned a series of attacks on guards. Court records show that the first target was to be a veteran sergeant, thirty-eight-year-old Howell Dean Burchfield, who was rumored to be supplying weapons to the Aryan Brotherhood, a rival prison gang. According to multiple BGF members, Jarvis wasn't told about the plot because of a rift he'd had with the planner of the attack. As a result, he didn't know what was coming the night of June 8 of that year: Sergeant Burchfield was taking the nightly prisoner count, a mundane chore that he'd repeated hundreds of times. An inmate called to him and asked for a light for his cigarette. When Burchfield approached the man's cell, the prisoner stabbed him with a makeshift spear, severing his pulmonary artery. By the time help arrived, the guard was dead.

That night and the following day, those suspected of involvement in the killing were moved from South Block's C-section, where they'd been confined, to the Adjustment Center. Jarvis apparently wasn't a suspect, because he was left alone. Prior to the murder he'd had unusual freedom of movement as a "tier tender," and that privilege continued. When other prisoners in the block were locked in their cells, Jarvis swept and mopped tiers, delivered dinner trays, and scrubbed supply room walls.

Six months later, Jarvis and other inmates were watching a football game when another prisoner yelled out for Jarvis to switch to a news channel. When he did, he saw his face alongside those of two other BGF members. A newscaster reported that the killers of the San Quentin correctional officer had been identified.

The next morning, Jarvis was moved to the AC, and a guard delivered a notice informing him that he was being charged with participating in the Burchfield murder. He suspected that he'd been framed by the same renegade gang member who planned the murder, because Jarvis was known to be a loyal soldier who wouldn't break the BGF code, which forbade speaking about any of the organization's members or activities. The price he paid for his loyalty was a charge for a crime with "special circumstances"—the killing of a police officer—that could result in his execution.

*   *   *

The murder trial began in 1989. On the mornings court was in session, Jarvis changed from prison denim into an orange jumpsuit. He was shackled with leg irons, handcuffs, and a chain around his waist and moved from his cell to a California Department of Corrections van, which took him to the blue-domed, Frank Lloyd Wright–designed Marin County Civic Center. He sat alongside his lawyers in a wood-paneled courtroom.

In preliminary hearings, Jarvis's attorneys filed a series of motions, but Marin County Superior Court justice Beverly Savitt ruled mostly against him. Then came jury selection, which was also inauspicious. Jarvis's attorneys quickly used up all their peremptory challenges. In the end, all but one juror was white, and all of them supported the death penalty.

Jarvis hunched in his chair while lawyers and witnesses talked about him as if he weren't there. Sometimes he looked up at the judge and saw kindness, almost motherly concern, but other times she looked right through him. He told Melody that the trial felt like "one nail in my coffin after another."

2

BREATHING, SITTING

After months of work on the mitigation report, Melody brought Jarvis a draft, which he read that night. When he finished, he was livid.

He wrote Melody a venomous diatribe: "You smile to my face and write about me like a dog. The police basically would have written the same things you wrote." He told her he never wanted to see her again.

Jarvis couldn't believe he'd trusted Melody. How many times did he have to learn he couldn't trust *anyone*?

Still boiling with rage, he picked up the report and read it again the next day. The further he read the worse he felt—hotter and angrier and sicker. Then, midway through, he had a horrifying epiphany: Melody hadn't turned against him. She'd done her job. She'd pieced together an accurate account of his life and reported the truth. The truth was what enraged him.

Melody described his mother as a prostitute who'd had men come to the house; her neglect; his father's violence, and then his father leaving. She reported his stepfather Otis's frequent beatings and the unremitting physical abuse Jarivs had endured in foster homes and state institutions.

Where was he in those stories? He'd been passive, hiding, afraid.

He'd spent his whole life proving that he wasn't a victim, but Melody's report showed that that was exactly what he was.

Jarvis sat on the bunk, reeling and nauseous. Then he thought about the vicious letter he'd sent Melody.

He wrote her again. "I have a tendency to react," he said. "Historically these kinds of reactions have been the worst mistakes I've made. . . . I'm fucking up. I apologize."

"I have a lot of trust in your better nature, Jarvis," Melody responded. "Your true self will always arise and open your heart. I know you'll be mad at me again—there are hard times coming—it's a hard and scary case. But if you stay committed, I will. I will never let you down."

Melody's letter calmed him. He was also relieved when he heard from Carlette. She, too, accepted his apology and said she'd visit soon.

* * *

Jarvis's relief was fleeting. The trial dragged on, and not only did he worry about the eventual judgment but also, every day, his survival. On the tier, he was vulnerable to the whims of guards, who weren't waiting for a verdict to punish him; they considered the charge enough proof that he'd been involved in the plot to kill their colleague. Guards ransacked his cell, ostensibly conducting random searches, and confiscated his few possessions. Once, an officer escorting Jarvis to the showers pushed him down a flight of stairs, professing that it was an accident.

Melody visited the day after the guard's assault, and she saw the anguish in Jarvis's eyes. She said to herself, "There has to be something I can do."

Back when Melody tore her Achilles tendon, a doctor recommended she try meditating to ease the pain. She attended a class and found that it did help. And something unexpected happened: memories of her troubled childhood flooded her mind. She recalled her mother grabbing her and shaking her violently. She relived losing her child and thought of her beloved baby sister, who had inherited the worst of their mother's depression. In spite of her own trauma, Melody had pulled it together, but her sister never did. One day while she was drunk, she fell, hit her head, and died. Melody never recovered from the loss.

Melody confided all that to a teacher at a Berkeley meditation center who taught her a technique he said could help her face her childhood trauma, accept her sister's death, and move on. He told her to meditate on the experiences from a safe distance and imagine them unfolding before her eyes. He told her to repeat the meditation often. "Over time, the memories lose their power," he promised.

Each morning when Melody meditated, she used the technique, and a lifetime of repressed grief erupted. She felt her sister's death and other losses. She watched her mother's violence. Over time, the memories *did* lose their power. Meditating helped her face and release the anger, guilt, and resentment she'd carried since childhood.

Recalling her experience, Melody suggested that Jarvis try meditating with her. "It's helping me," she said. "Maybe it'll help you."

Jarvis looked at her in disbelief. "That's what you got for me? In *this* place? They're trying to kill me, and you want me to *meditate*?"

They let the subject drop, but on another visit, Jarvis looked fatigued and miserable. He stared down at his hands, balled into fists. They sat in silence for a while until Jarvis spoke so softly that Melody could barely hear him. He looked at her and asked if she really thought "that meditation shit" could help.

"It might," she said. "I think it can. As I said, it's helping me. Can we just try?" She instructed him: "All you do is sit quietly with a straight spine, close your eyes, breathe, and pay attention to your breath as it flows in and out. That's all. Just feel your chest rise when you breathe in, and feel it fall when you breathe out. When your mind wanders, return your attention to your breath."

Jarvis looked up at her with fire in his eyes. "*Sit*? Close my *eyes*? Are you out of your goddamn mind?"

She didn't understand.

"If you want to survive in here, you *don't* close your eyes," he said. "You want to see *everything*. Your life depends on it. And you *do not sit.*

On the yard, you are always ready to defend yourself. When you're sitting, you have no legs."

"I get it," Melody said, "but no one will know. You'll be hidden in your cell."

He countered, "You don't understand. This isn't just about where I am but who I am. I do not sit. I do not close my eyes."

She let him calm down for a moment, and she said, "Maybe you can try. Just try. We'll sit here for five minutes. That's all. Just breathe deep and slow, slowly in, and slowly out."

He was no less comfortable closing his eyes, but he wanted to please Melody, because he still worried that she'd abandon him. He didn't say anything, but he did close his eyes. He opened them and looked around warily, then closed them again and took a breath.

Nights were hardest. "Sleep doesn't come when you live surrounded by wall-to-wall enemies and the threat of poison gas filling your lungs," he wrote Melody.

When he did fall asleep, Jarvis had nightmares. In one dream, he was in the gas chamber. He'd seen pictures of the room, steel like a diving bell or space module, sea green, with hermetically sealed hatches and thick glass portholes. He was strapped down and awaiting the poison. Petrified, he looked over at the executioner. Jarvis focused on the man's face. It was his own.

Jarvis tried to meditate in his cell. There wasn't much space in the four-and-a-half-by-ten-and-a-half-foot rectangle, but between the bed and toilet he found room to place a folded blanket on the floor.

He sat straight with his legs crossed, closed his eyes, and breathed. When his mind wandered, he brought it back to his breath. He was unsure if he was doing it right. In spite of the blanket, the floor was hard and cold.

He was distracted by the noise on the tier and the chatter in his head. What were the cons shouting about? What slop would be served for dinner? He fixated on the trial: he envisioned being convicted, sentenced, and executed.

When Jarvis described the experience to Melody, she repeated advice from her teacher that had helped her: "When those thoughts come, gently push them away." Jarvis tried that technique. He had a literal image of pushing the bad thoughts away. "I don't need *you*," he said as he swept one aside. "I don't need you," when another came. He made it through five minutes. Then ten. He tried it the next morning and the next.

He found that meditation calmed him. However, sometimes when he meditated, instead of serenity he felt panic. His heart would pound, and his breathing would quicken. Sometimes he saw and felt things like in a nightmare. Monsters, roaches, and the screams of deranged cons filled his head. He thought of the men in San Quentin—his neighbors. He thought of their crimes. They were men who'd lit their parents on fire, raped, cut up victims. He was almost choking, gasping for breath.

He decided to quit. But he didn't. He tried again. He breathed in and breathed out. At first he did it for Melody, but he continued for himself. He was scared and enraged—and desperate—and he didn't know what else he could do to try to cope.

Melody repeated another instruction from her teacher: "When you begin to panic, picture the upsetting events and feel the uncomfortable feelings from a safe distance. Instead of being inside them, you can watch them come. If you watch them come, you can watch them go." The teacher had said to remember that "fear is a thought, and thoughts can't hurt you. Thoughts can't kill you."

Sometimes Jarvis glimpsed the profundity of that advice, but holding on to it was like trying to hold on to water. Melody assured him that understanding would come, and her prescription was always the same: practice.

He did practice. He'd go to a dark place—his chest would pound—but if he remembered to concentrate on his breath, his heart slowed. When fear flooded him, if he recalled the teacher's words—"Fear is a thought, and thoughts can't hurt you"—the fear lessened.

Occasionally Jarvis emerged from meditation feeling energized. It made him feel . . . what? It made him feel—the thought startled him—better than he'd ever felt before in his life. He was on trial for murder and could be condemned, yet he felt a lightness and optimism that would last throughout the morning.

And so he kept going.

Every morning. Roused himself. Folded the blanket and placed it on the floor. Sat with his legs crossed. Corrected his posture, straightening his spine.

Inhaled.

Slowly.

Concentrated on the air as it filled his lungs, and, when his lungs were full, held in the air, feeling it swirl inside, and then, slowly, slowly, let it flow out.

Sometimes he tried to meditate but couldn't concentrate on his breath or still his mind. Then anger welled up inside him again: the unfairness, the betrayal, his inability to speak out.

He sometimes felt like a fool to even try. Once he thought dismissively, "I may be sentenced to death, and I'm sitting here *breathing?*"

But he pondered that notion for a moment more, and it transformed itself in an extraordinary way: *I may be sentenced to death, and I'm sitting here breathing!* He felt something like hope.

But the hope would inevitably evaporate. Awful thoughts beset him: terror about the result of the trial and fear of reprisals by guards. Jarvis viewed depression as a weakness—it was a word he'd never abide—but he fell into depression so deep and dark he felt he'd never emerge.

Melody passed along more advice from her teacher: "Remember, Jarvis. None of that is today. Come back to now. You can control your mind."

You can control your mind. Those words triggered a memory of the time he'd heard them before.

"We will train your body and train your mind."

That's what Jarvis was told once he'd been inducted into the BGF.

There was boot camp–like physical training that included calisthenics, jogging around the yard, and martial arts. The soldiers spent hours marching. As they did, they repeated in marching cadence a drill instructor's words. The instructor yelled, "Can't stop," and the recruits repeated, "Can't stop!"

It continued:

"Can't stop."

"Won't stop!"

"Never cop."

"Never cop!"

"Never drop."

"Never drop!"

"Who say?"

"We say!"

"Machine."

"Machine!"

"Machine on the move."

"Machine on the move!"

"Machine we never lose."

"Machine we never lose!"

"Over the wall."

"Over the wall!"

"Freedom call."

"Freedom call!"

The voices of sixty black men yelling those words echoed throughout San Quentin—in the chow hall, on the north and south yards, and up in the warden's office.

The training intensified. Jarvis practiced taking dictation in Swahili and English and learned how to fashion knives, zip guns, and explosives. His responsibilities included copying and delivering kites—coded messages—from one BGF member to another. He was charged with monitoring the tier and passing contraband between members.

The instructors also trained his mind. He was schooled in the history of the BGF, the Nation of Islam, and the Black Panther Party. He studied BGF doctrine, its constitution, and its code of conduct.

Jarvis told Melody that the training had succeeded in politicizing him and giving him purpose he'd never had, but it also trained him to feel nothing. He'd been hard, but it made him harder.

Jarvis became lost in thought. When he spoke again, he said he realized that his training for the gang had actually begun at birth. Throughout his life, he'd been taught to take punishment and give it while silencing his conscience, concealing his fear, and suppressing his will. But now he was engaged in an utterly different type of mental training, and he was starting to feel its effects. He felt a chill travel through his body when he realized he was twenty-four years old, in prison, facing a murder charge that could result in his death. But he was in training again.

3

SCARS

Besides writing for her job, Melody wrote essays about the criminal justice system for magazines and journals. On one visit she showed Jarvis a story she'd written about children visiting their parents in prison. He responded thoughtfully, and his reaction gave her an idea. She was continuing to flesh out the report about his life and asked if he'd help her by writing answers to questions she would provide.

Jarvis had never learned to read or write well, but when he was twelve or thirteen years old, a teacher at a program for juvenile offenders had him write a story and told him that he had a talent for writing. Other than in letters, he'd never written for or about himself. He was insecure about his limited vocabulary and poor grammar, but he agreed to try. He took Melody's questions to his cell and answered them truthfully.

When she read his responses, Melody saw his talent, too.

She was in a women's writers group in which she and friends did writing exercises, and she suggested that they do a couple of those exercises together. They agreed on a theme—"rain," for instance, or "a conversation overheard." She took off her watch and lay it on the small shelf between them in the booth. "All right," she said. "Ten minutes. Go."

She took his exercises to her writers group's meetings, and she returned to San Quentin with the other group members' feedback. Jarvis became a de facto member of the group, the only male and the only prisoner.

Jarvis began writing in his cell. He wrote with the Bic pen insert, which was, he told Melody, his most valuable possession. Not having a table or desk, he rolled up his mattress and stuffed it in a corner, then sat cross-legged on the floor, placed a sheet of paper on the stripped concrete slab that was his bed, and wrote feverishly for hours. Paper was at a premium; in order to get as many words on each page as possible, he developed a tiny, even script that looked almost like typing. Sometimes he wrote all night. He never imagined there was something he could be good at, a talent, and being inspired to do something constructive—being inspired at all—was a new feeling. Writing gave him a different kind of power than came from knives or guns—subtler but no less palpable.

"You meet a whole new person when you start writing about yourself," he wrote Melody.

Writing opened him to strange feelings and memories he'd lost, including many he didn't want to remember.

"I see how messed up I was, believe me," he told her. "Some of my past experiences were like a horror movie."

Writing not only made Jarvis remember more, it made him notice more. He felt the wind on his skin when it found its way to him through a broken window across the walkway from his cell. He heard the sorrowful cries of gulls, and he relished the soothing warmth of the sun on his face when he was on the yard for the all-too-brief three hours, three times a week he was allowed outside. He noticed light and shadows moving along his cell walls and floor. He eavesdropped on conversations among inmates and guards. He studied their accents and vernacular, and he recorded their dialogue.

Jarvis noticed sounds he'd lived with but never heard: the scrape of a food cart's wheels along the corridor, the jangling rhythm of keys and handcuffs clanging off the belts of guards who passed his cell, the scurry of a mouse, and the babel of radio stations tuned to country, metal, and blues, wailing preachers and NPR.

That heightened awareness filtered into his meditation. He noticed his surroundings: feelings, noises, smells. But even more intensely, he felt a new world of sensation inside his body. He discovered the tightness in his belly, the alternating tautness and slack of his lungs, the stress that throbbed in his temples, the pulsing weight of anxiety in his chest.

When he described those sensations to Melody, she said he was discovering mindfulness, a form of meditation. "You become fully present in the moment. Experience it. When your mind wanders, return to your body, what you sense outside and inside you, and breathe."

Jarvis's self-imposed training began each day with two hours of meditation followed by exercise. He recorded his progress on a calendar he'd drawn. Four hundred sit-ups, five hundred push-ups, five hundred or more burpees, and again. Next he walked up and down the length of his cell 520 times, which was a mile. That or he ran in place until the guard came by with the food cart with breakfast: cardboardy pancakes or powdered scrambled eggs, a couple slices of bread, and a packet of instant coffee that he mixed with lukewarm water from the sink.

On weekends or other times court wasn't in session, the morning routine was followed by writing letters and responses to more of Melody's questions, games of chess with other cons on the tier (they yelled moves, which they tracked in their respective cells), and reading. The few cherished hours he was allowed outside, he went to the yard to breathe clean air.

One day, Jarvis was on the yard, watching a group of shirtless men lifting weights. Though it was a common sight, he'd never paid attention to it before. He'd never noticed how their bodies were marked with scars, the evidence of whips, belts, chains, knives, bullets, and fire. It reminded him of slaves' scarred bodies, which he'd seen in old photographs in books, and of his own scars.

With sadness, he realized that all of those men had endured abuse and pain like his, and some had survived far worse. When he was alone with them on the yard, he cautiously asked them about their scars. Some shut him down, but others talked openly. One told him about how his father thrashed him with a steel rod. Another's father used a tire iron.

Jarvis's own scars had mostly faded, but one on his left forearm was prominent. Back when he was a teenager in a lockup for juvenile delinquents, counselors put lit cigarettes on boys' arms and bet on which of them would let the cigarette burn the longest without pulling away. Losers were beaten.

Later, when Jarvis told Melody about his conversations on the yard, she encouraged him to write them down.

He huddled over a sheet of paper and scratched a line at a time. "Deep sadness came over me as I watched these powerful men lift hundreds of pounds of weights over their heads," he wrote. "I looked around the yard and made the gruesome discovery that everyone else had the same deep gashes—behind their legs, on their backs, all over their ribs—evidence of the violence in our lives. . . .

"The histories of all of us in San Quentin were so similar, it was as if we had the same parents."

A few weeks later he gave Melody a half dozen pages and shifted uncomfortably while she read.

She marveled at his story. Beyond the solid writing, she saw it as a remarkable testament to how far he'd come since they'd met. Then he'd had no self-awareness, never mind the ability to see others. He cared about no one and nothing but himself. Now he recognized others' suffering, responded with compassion, and connected others' pain with his own.

Melody had a thought that made her smile. On his own and without knowing it, Jarvis had arrived at the heart of Buddhism.

Many prisoners find solace in religion, but Jarvis was disdainful of it after a lifetime of abuse in the name of God. He did have one positive memory of faith because of his first foster parents. When he was five years old and separated from his family, a social worker took him to live with Mamie and Dennis Procks, an elderly, childless couple who greeted his arrival with joy. They showed him around their freshly painted home on a quiet, tree-lined street where kids played and rode bikes. He was stunned when they showed him his room. When he lived with his mother, he shared a tiny room with his siblings and slept on a pee-stained mattress. At the Prockes' he had his own room, a dresser stocked with clean clothes, a closet full of toys, and his own bed with ironed sheets.

Every night before bed, Mamie made him pray. When she had him pray for his mother, Jarvis asked why. Mamie said his mother loved him, and it was hard for her to be separated from him. She got Jarvis talking about Cynthia, what he missed about her. Mamie told him to pray for Cynthia because she'd been through hard times. He missed his mother and sometimes felt angry that she wasn't around. He didn't understand why she left or where she had gone. When he thought about it, he felt sorry for himself. But Mamie made him feel sorry for *her*.

Whereas the Procks embodied generosity and Christlike goodness, Jarvis's subsequent foster parents proselytized about Jesus's love and dragged him to church, meanwhile beating and starving him. Judges invoked Christ as they issued cruel sentences. One exhorted him, "Look to Jesus in your heart," before sending him to a youth detention center "to get some discipline," which apparently meant being burned, beaten, and forced to fight other kids.

Melody and Jarvis had discussed religion, and she knew that he had good reason to be wary of it. She'd felt the same way until her meditation teacher helped her face the hurt she'd suffered because of her violent parents and the loss of her sister. Learning from Buddhist stories didn't require belief in the faith's core tenets, such as reincarnation and karma, but the parables inspired her. Along with meditation, studying Buddhism helped her heal.

Jarvis appreciated that Melody wasn't a blind follower, and he was intrigued when she said that Buddhist parables "make us think in new ways and break us out of the thought patterns that cause our suffering."

She sent him a book about Buddhist philosophy. One night he picked it up and read about the Buddha's previous life as a young prince named Siddhartha Gautama, who, walking in a forest, came across a tigress who was starving and couldn't feed her cubs. The prince gave his body to the tigress to save her and the cubs from dying.

The story's moral of compassion and generosity didn't quite resonate with Jarvis. He thought, *Now, that's some stupid shit. He died to save some tigers?*

*　　*　　*

33

As the trial continued, Melody encouraged Jarvis and the lawyers reassured him, saying the truth would come out, but whatever optimism and bravado he had was fading. He tried not to think about the worst of the possible outcomes of the trial, but he couldn't keep them away. Forget about getting out and going home, having a normal life. Forget about being with Carlette or his other siblings and their families, watching their children grow up, having Sunday dinners with them, having his *own* family. The possibility of a murder conviction was sinking in, and so was the fact that he could die here. One of those nights spent awake, freaking out, scared, careening from hopelessness to panic to rage and back, he imagined himself being locked in the gas chamber. His temples pounded so hard he thought he'd pass out. Meditation helped him find moments of relative peace, but it wasn't enough to pull him out of waking nightmares like that one. He fell deeper into depression, feeling he'd never get out. In the morning he wrote Melody and admitted that he sometimes contemplated suicide. "I won't do it," he wrote. "Don't worry. But you couldn't be in here and not think about it."

Guards continued to provoke him. He knew they hoped he'd fight back so they'd have an excuse to beat him. Most of the time he was able to restrain himself, but sometimes they pushed him too far. Once he cursed at a pair of guards and was dragged to the end of the tier and thrown into what the prison called a "quiet cell." Behind two steel doors, the section housed some of San Quentin's most violent and insane prisoners and was like a lockdown ward in a mental hospital. Prisoners moaned, wept, howled, and screamed all night long. Jarvis felt like screaming along with them. Lying on his bunk, he held his hands over his ears and fought the urge to cry.

*   *   *

Meditation provided some relief from the horrors of the quiet cell. Jarvis also bided his time exercising maniacally and, when he could concentrate, writing letters and reading, until he was moved back to his previous Adjustment Center cell three months later.

Late that spring, the jury began deliberations. While waiting for a verdict, Jarvis was kept in a holding tank near the courtroom. One day when Melody visited, she gave him a pamphlet with a picture of an ancient man on the cover. He had a wizened face, a long, wispy mustache and beard, wild wiry eyebrows, and eyes that seemed to stare directly at him. The accompanying text offered free writings by the "lama" Chagdud Tulku Rinpoche. Jarvis wrote to the address and requested them. In a note, he described himself as a prisoner who'd been accused of a murder he hadn't committed. If he was convicted, he could be sentenced to death. He said he'd been meditating regularly but admitted that with the trial hanging over him and his having to watch out for threatening guards, he was struggling to continue.

That evening when Jarvis was back in his cell, he handed a guard the letter to be mailed, and he didn't give it any more thought. At the time, he was trying *not* to think, especially about the pending verdict. He tried to remain positive—he was innocent, so of course he'd be exonerated—but he'd sat through damning testimony and tried to brace himself in case the news was bad.

The trial continued for two agonizing years. Finally Jarvis was told that the jury had reached its decision, and he was led from the holding cell to the courtroom.

He appeared stoic when he and his lawyers were told to rise, and the judge asked the foreman if the jury had reached a verdict. The foreman said they had.

They'd found him guilty.

Jarvis had rehearsed the moment in his mind, but it still didn't seem possible.

The judge announced that the trial would next move to the sentencing phase, and Jarvis was taken back to his cell, where he lay down and closed his eyes. When he opened them, he spiraled downward into a black rage from which no amount of meditation, no teachings, no parable could lift him.

The penalty phase began and, as expected, the prosecution argued for Jarvis's death. His lawyers used witnesses Melody had tracked down in their presentation, determined to convince the jurors to spare his life. They hoped that the testimony of those who knew Jarvis when he was young, the accounts of the violence and abandonment he'd endured as a child and teenager, would convince the jury that he shouldn't be executed. It would also be the first time Jarvis would speak in court.

Prepared by the lawyers, he read a statement Melody had helped him compose. When he finished reading it, he answered lawyers' questions about his years of incarceration. He was forthright except when asked about the Black Guerrilla Family. The BGF code of conduct didn't expire, and Jarvis remained loyal and refused to speak about the gang. When he declined to debrief about the BGF, Judge Savitt ordered that his entire testimony be stricken from the record and that the jurors disregard what he had said.

After he testified, Jarvis was consumed with guilt over what he'd revealed about his mother's neglect and abuse. He felt he'd betrayed her by telling family secrets. Though Melody reassured him that he'd done the right thing, he was still distraught.

Melody thought it might help him if he wrote Cynthia a letter. She knew, and Jarvis did, too, how writing could clarify one's thinking. Though Cynthia was dead, Melody suggested that Jarvis write to her as if she were alive.

"Dear Mama," he wrote, "[In court,] I did what I know you would have wanted me to do, which is held my head up as I told what I had been through. If I said anything that hurt you more than it hurt me, then I am sorry that your rest is still with pain."

He listed ways she had hurt him, how she'd used him to "jack up the price for sex" by telling men "I gotta take care of my kids" and never thought about the fact that he and the other children heard her with men in the bedroom. He asked why she didn't intervene when Otis [his mother's boyfriend] hit him and his siblings.

Jarvis asked, "Did you love Otis more than us . . . even when he pimped you like a dog?"

Jarvis wrote about how he felt when she was high: "I used to watch you lying on the bed. . . . I always felt like you were Mama when you were asleep and a stranger when you were awake. . . .

Mama, we all were scared of you. Nobody knows how you whipped us. Nobody knows the many things drugs made you do."

But then he softened: "Sometimes my thoughts tell me that I should hate you too, but life showed you so much hate that when I look into your eyes in my memories of you, you were like a little girl needing someone—needing a father just like we all did."

He concluded, "Mama, I have to confront these memories—they're killing me. . . . I will hate everything that killed you. We share the same hurt, Mama, but I just can't grow old hurting the way I do. I have to surrender to it—let it go, make sense of it all. Mama, I know you loved me and I swear I love you. Please forgive me and [don't] hold me to blame [for what I said in court]. It's not a secret when horror lives and exists in the mind. But shit, now I'm scared of you and this feeling of guilt is why I write to you for your forgiveness."

He signed it "JJ—3:58 AM."

His letter broke Melody's heart. Jarvis was apologizing to his mother, but what he needed was an apology *from* her, something he would never get.

The penalty phase continued for three weeks. Besides Jarvis, relatives, former counselors, and foster parents spoke about his difficult early life, testimony meant to induce the jury's sympathy. However, the prosecution argued that Jarvis's life history didn't excuse his criminality; it documented it.

Prosecutors once again emphasized Jarvis's long record, his violence at LA County Jail, and his write-ups in San Quentin for fighting and other crimes for which he'd never been charged or convicted. Unlike in the guilt phase, they were allowed to raise unsubstantiated accusations; the innocent-until-proven-guilty presumption had ended when he'd been convicted. They portrayed him as coldhearted and unremorseful, but it was still shocking when the jury sentenced him to death.

The final stage of the trial came next. Judges in death penalty cases can affirm or modify juries' recommendations based on their own evaluation of the evidence.

Jarvis's legal team believed that his life would be spared, especially since the lives of the other convicted defendants—the man who stabbed the guard and the one who ordered the killing—had been; they'd been sentenced to life in prison without the possibility of parole.

Judge Savitt spent a month completing a review before summoning Jarvis to court to hear her decision in July 1990.

Michael Satris, a renowned criminal lawyer, made the final plea. He stood and spoke with somber eloquence as he implored Judge Savitt to try to "live the experience of Jarvis Masters . . . to walk the life that Jarvis did: be shaken in the womb by the violence that literally was awaiting his birth, and to be born in that brutality, and be abandoned, and be rejected, and be in the ghetto, and feel that pain, and feel that shame."

He asked the judge to consider Jarvis's life from there, after being removed from his mother's custody and separated from his sisters, who were the only consistent family he'd had, "to be isolated, and cry those tears."

Satris described Jarvis's entry into foster care; after the Procks, it was a "world of violence and crime," which in turn led to one cruel institution after another.

And then to San Quentin and solitary confinement. "We know what the conditions of that confinement can do to a person.

"What's remarkable," Satris continued, "is the way that he has been able to break through that violence even with the limited resources and opportunity he's had. And he *has* broken through. And there is the evidence which supports the long-standing program of maturation, rehabilitation, development, whatever you want to call it, that has allowed Mr. Masters to break through that. And how strong, how invincible is the human spirit that any of us, our children, that we can have such confidence that we would have been able to withstand the conditions, the effects of Mr. Masters's upbringing on him any better than he has been able to do?"

Satris closed by imploring the judge to "reach as deep" into herself as she could to modify the jury's sentence and spare Jarvis's life.

Next, the prosecution argued that the evidence of mitigation was outweighed by the "evidence for aggravation." Once again the prosecution listed the armed robberies for which Jarvis had been convicted and claimed that he'd participated in the violent crimes they'd raised earlier, and then its presentation ended. It was Judge Savitt's turn.

The judge began by admitting that there had been "fleeting" moments during the trial when she had asked herself why she had taken on the case in the first place. She also stated her opposition to the death penalty but said she was charged with applying the law whether she agreed with it or not. "It's my duty."

She then addressed Satris directly. "You've turned Mr. Masters . . . into a human being," she said. "He was born into hell. He was born for reasons that are almost impossible for me to comprehend. If people don't want children, they shouldn't have them. Apparently, his mother didn't know how not to have them."

Savitt acknowledged that it had been a tragedy when Jarvis was taken away from the Procks. That was when "he gave up on himself," she said, "and that is when he became a very destructive person." Then he entered the prison system, "another hell."

Savitt took a breath. When she continued, she said something that stunned Jarvis. She claimed that she understood him to a large degree, "the best that one who was raised white middle-class can understand," and then proceeded to address the aggravating circumstances.

As evidence against him, she cited violence in Jarvis's past, including the robberies. She also cited his refusal to debrief about the BGF, believing that his refusal contradicted his claims that he'd renounced the gang.

"Mr. Masters," she said, "will you please stand."

Jarvis stood.

Over the previous two years, he had sometimes glimpsed warmth in the judge's face. Now whatever sympathy he'd seen or imagined was replaced by hardness.

"It is the order of this court that you shall suffer the death penalty," she said. "Said penalty to be inflicted within the walls of the state prison at San Quentin, California, in the manner prescribed by law."

PART TWO

THE SECOND NOBLE TRUTH

THE CAUSE OF SUFFERING

God whispers to us in our pleasures, speaks in our conscience, but shouts in our pains: it is his megaphone to rouse a deaf world.

—C. S. Lewis

4

CONDEMNED

The guards were quiet on the ride from the courthouse, but noise erupted when the van entered the prison. Jarvis heard car horns and guards cheering. Through the mesh-covered windows he saw COs giving one another the thumbs-up. They were celebrating his death sentence.

Jarvis was led from the van to his cell. Late that night he heard footsteps and then pounding. He looked up into the blinding beams of flashlights held by guards, one of whom told him to step up to the bars. Jarvis thought they were there to kill him. Mob justice. A lynching. Shielding his eyes with his hands, trembling, he rose and stumbled forward.

"We have to read this," a guard snapped. "You have to sign it."

They weren't there to kill him, after all, but to carry out the mandatory reading of the execution order. Jarvis signed the piece of paper that condemned him to die.

The next morning, breakfast was delivered as usual, and the day progressed as if nothing had changed. Also as usual, the mail was delivered in the evening. Jarvis examined a large envelope from someone named Lisa Leghorn, who in a note explained that she was an assistant and interpreter to Chagdud Tulku Rinpoche, the Buddhist lama Jarvis had written to months before. Leghorn wrote that Rinpoche was glad that Jarvis had reached out to him, and she referred to a small book in the package entitled *Life in Relation to Death*, which contained a transcript of a talk by the lama. "Read it," she said. "See if it speaks to you."

Jarvis picked the book up and was instantly transfixed. On the first page, the lama described death as a subject people often ignore or think about frivolously, as if it were no big deal. Then the author wrote, "This is a nice theory until one is dying. Then experience and theory differ." He continued, "Then one is powerless and everything familiar is lost. One is overwhelmed by a great turbulence of fear, disorientation, and confusion. For this reason it is essential to prepare well in advance for the moment when the mind and body separate."

Jarvis closed the book and breathed deeply. A familiar, choking emotion welled up in him: anguish. But he read on. The teacher said that all people should prepare for death, and one approach was to picture the ways they might die. He listed an airplane crash, an automobile accident, a terminal illness, and being stabbed by a mugger. He didn't mention the gas chamber.

Another approach was called "meditative contemplations." Jarvis read through them quickly until he got to one that made him shudder. People should ask themselves two questions every night before bed: "If I die tonight in my sleep . . . What have I done with my life? Have I been of benefit or have I caused harm?"

Jarvis needed no time to ponder his answer. He knew that he'd benefited no one and he'd caused immeasurable harm.

He read all night. Dawn was breaking as he turned the final page, but he was wide awake. He didn't believe in omens, but he reeled at the thought that during his first day on death row, the mail had brought him a guide to dying.

Jarvis penned a response to Chagdud Tulku and the translator, thanking them for the package and explaining what had happened since he'd first written, that he'd been given the death penalty. He told them he had been trying to get his mind around the sentence. He admitted that he was afraid.

Prison mail was slow, and it took a month for him to hear back from the lama, who said he understood Jarvis's confusion and fear but assured him that he was fortunate; his situation was a gift. "You can use your circumstances for your betterment and to benefit others," he said. The thought appalled Jarvis. Being on death row was no gift.

The lama wrote that all people have been sentenced to death—in that way, Jarvis wasn't unique. That idea angered Jarvis, too. Yes, he thought, everyone is going to die, but not everyone is living a hundred yards from the site of their execution.

"We all live in a prison, and we all hold the key," Chagdud Tulku wrote. *More patronizing bullshit*, Jarvis thought. *You do not live in prison. I live in prison. You may have a key, but the keys to my cell are hanging off my jailers' belts.*

Jarvis's anger diminished when the lama offered concrete instructions: "Stick with meditation, because it allows us to gain insight into own our mind and its projections. Fear is in your mind. Regret is in your mind." That advice recalled Melody's teacher's description of fear as "just a thought," which had helped him in the past.

The key, the teacher said, was practice. Jarvis should meditate at least twice a day, even when it was difficult. He said he should allow himself to feel doubt, confusion, anger, and fear. "It's normal for you to feel that way." Finally, the lama said, "If you need help we're here for you. You are like family now."

A new family. When Jarvis read that word, the last remnants of his anger melted away.

Jarvis tried to follow the lama's instructions, but his despair only worsened over the following months. His friends and lawyers visited and tried to bolster him. The lawyers said that the trial had been a travesty, and they assured him he'd win on appeal. Kelly Hayden, a legal assistant who'd become a friend, visited and commiserated with him. She believed that his conviction and sentence were racist, and she said so. She said, "Don't take it personally." They exchanged horrified looks and burst out laughing. It was a brief moment of levity.

Those first days, Jarvis obsessed about the death sentence and became preoccupied with the message inherent in the judge's words before she'd condemned him: "If people don't want children, they shouldn't have them. Apparently, his mother didn't know how not to have them." He turned those words over in his mind: *If my mother shouldn't have had me, I should never have been born; the world would have been a better place without me.*

Those words affirmed his worst feelings about himself, a message reinforced since he was a child. The judge had seen into his soul. He had been born useless. Those who saw him as evil were right.

Carlette came, but there was little either of them could say. She sobbed and left.

He tried to reread *Life in Relation to Death*, but he couldn't bear it.

In a letter to Chagdud Tulku, Jarvis admitted that he was falling into "the darkest place" and didn't know if he'd ever be able to pull himself out. The lama had said that he and Lisa were there for him if he needed help. Jarvis needed help badly now, and he asked for it.

In her response, Lisa suggested that they talk in person, and he readily agreed. A month later, when her application was approved, she came to San Quentin.

Jarvis had expected a Tibetan like the lama in the photograph, but Lisa looked like a flower child or gypsy. She wasn't a cold and detached Buddhist scholar; she was open and kind and funny.

After some small talk, Lisa said that she and Rinpoche understood his despair and the difficulty of meditating in that state. "Yes, it's hard, but it can save you. Meditation is hardest when we're most afraid, because it forces us to face our fears when all we want to do is run from them. But it's the only way out of our misery.

"It's hard to see that where you are," she acknowledged, "but it's like walking from one mountain to another. If you think about how far you have to go, you'll freeze up and never take the first step. Just take the step."

"I would," Jarvis said. "I can't. I try."

He broached something that had been gnawing at him: "In these books I see pictures of Buddhists sitting in robes on mountain peaks, chanting in these gardens with white flowers and blue skies. Maybe that works there, but how in the world am I going to sit in this hellhole praying to some stone fat man? I live with rapists and killers. Everyone talks about enlightenment, living in the light. But I live in hell."

Lisa responded with a parable about a woman named Kisa Gotami who had lived at the time of the Buddha. Her son died, and she was overcome with grief. Carrying his lifeless body, she set off in search of the Buddha. After many days, she found him and pled with him to bring her child back to life. The Buddha said he'd make a medicine that would revive him, but it required a special ingredient, mustard seeds that came from a home that hadn't been touched by suffering. He sent Kisa Gotami to find some.

She went from village to village and house to house, knocking on door after door. People pitied her and were happy to help, but the seeds they offered were useless, because every person she met had suffered.

She went to more villages and visited more homes, but none had escaped suffering. She was desperate when she reached the thousandth door. She knocked, and a woman answered. Once again she begged for mustard seeds. The woman had some, but then Kisa Gotami asked if she'd experienced suffering in her life. The woman looked up at her. Her life had been filled with suffering.

Kisa Gotami wept. She wasn't crying for herself but for everyone she'd met. She understood at last what the Buddha had wanted her to see, that no one escapes suffering and no one escapes death. She had experienced what she needed to in order to get past her grief. She felt compassion for others. In Lisa's telling, the instant Kisa Gotami felt that, she grasped the universality of suffering and the impermanence of life. She understood that her son had joined the vast pool of souls who have lived and died. She understood that in her suffering she was like all humans. She accepted her son's death, and she was freed from her pain. She became awakened and attained the state of enlightenment as a person who grasped the true nature of existence.

Jarvis was quiet. He'd heard and read other Buddhist stories, but this one touched him differently for some reason.

A moment later, a guard rapped on the door, ending the visit.

That night, Jarvis lay on his cot listening to the prison's unceasing noise: sobs like crying wind, coughing, hacking, and the footsteps of guards. After having been unable to meditate for months, he moved to the floor, crossed his legs, and sat erect. He inhaled as deeply as he ever had.

In a dreamlike state, he saw a man sitting in meditation, his body engulfed in flames. He focused on the meditator and recognized him. The man was himself. As if he were watching through a telephoto lens, he panned back from inside his cell to the tier. Somehow he saw inside the other cells, each containing a man who was also on fire. He zoomed out more and saw San Quentin from the sky. From that vantage, he saw several thousand burning bodies. Still higher, from the clouds, he saw houses across the Bay Area burning. Then he saw California, which was also engulfed in flames. Higher. The country. Then the continent, and then the Western Hemisphere. Next he was watching from space. From that height he saw the whole planet floating in blackness. The water was blue. The landmasses were brown and green. On those expanses, wherever there were humans, fires burned.

Jarvis returned to the prison, to the thousands of men in cages unfit for animals. He thought of Kisa Gotami and realized that suffering was all around him—everywhere humans were. When he opened his eyes, he was shaking, and tears were streaming down his cheeks.

5

AWAKENING

Some San Quentin buildings were a century and a half old. When it rained or the fog was dense, water leaked from ceilings and dripped down walls. Those days passed slowly, one drip at a time.

When Jarvis first tried meditation, he couldn't sit for five minutes, but eventually he was able to sit for two hours or more. However, since the overwhelming experience of seeing—*feeling*—the ubiquity of humanity's pain, he'd stopped again.

"I can't," he told Melody. "I'm tired. It's too much."

"What's going on?" she asked.

"I just don't have it in me."

Melody responded, "I think maybe you're afraid," and she reminded Jarvis of her own introduction to meditation. "Sitting there,

53

facing the pain, was the hardest thing I'd ever done," she said. "I wanted to run, but"—she paused—"the thing is, waking up hurts." She added, "It's normal to be afraid. Keep going. There's an old saying, 'The only way out is through,' and it's true."

Jarvis was no less apprehensive, but he forced himself onto the floor that night. He assumed the lotus position, closed his eyes, and drew in the deepest breath he could. He exhaled and breathed in again, and he kept going—even when he felt the urge to stop.

His attention moved to his body. He noticed how fast his heart was beating, how tense he was. He examined the underlying feeling—it *was* fear. But what was he afraid of?

He felt it burning, the fire he'd witnessed. It would consume him if he went back to that terrifying place. He remembered the techniques Melody had taught him, and he tried to push away the image of the burning bodies, but he couldn't. Once again he watched a body in flames and saw it as his.

His instinct was to flee, but he planted his feet and stood his ground. He looked closer and saw that it wasn't a man in flames but a child. He looked even closer and saw that the child was *him*. Jarvis walked toward the burning child and entered its body.

He was four or five years old, before the state took him from his family, and he and his sisters were playing. Cynthia rushed in, yelling at the children, "Pack your things!" but it was too late. The door banged open, and Cynthia shoved the kids under her bed, whispering urgently, "Don't you dare move a muscle."

Jarvis heard a man's voice. "Where are they?" he demanded. "I am going to kill you and kill those kids."

Then heavy shoes stomped into the room. Jarvis heard his mother bellow "No!" and he saw his father's hard black shoes moving toward Cynthia. Then he heard her wretched screams. He watched her being dragged out of the room and then heard crashing dishes, thuds, and her whimpering. Finally the front door slammed. There was silence and then the quiet sound of a person dragging herself along the floor and into the bedroom. From under the bed, Jarvis saw his mother look at her children, making sure they were okay. Her face was covered in blood.

Reliving the experience, Jarvis trembled, and then he remembered the technique he'd learned. "I don't want you," he said as he tried to sweep the image aside. The panic subsided somewhat, but when he emerged from the meditation he'd broken out in a cold sweat.

Over the following months, when he meditated he returned to other memories. His mother's boyfriend, Otis, moved into the house after his father left for good. Cynthia said to call him his stepfather. Otis was playing with him, crawling on the floor, and they wrestled and boxed. It was all in fun, so why was Jarvis afraid? The pretend fighting turned serious, and Otis's hand reared back, swung forward, and slapped him across his face. Jarvis's ears rang, and he tasted blood. He looked up and saw Otis coming toward him again, this time holding an electrical cord. He felt the sting. One, two, three, four, five lashes. Otis said, "Don't you cry, or you'll get it twice as hard."

Another time Jarvis looked down at the bright face of his baby brother, whom he held in his arms. Cynthia and Otis had had twins, and she must have been aware of her limitations as a mother because she told Jarvis and his older sister, Charlene, that the babies were theirs to take care of. The girl, Carlette, was Charlene's; the boy, Carl, was Jarvis's.

Jarvis devoted himself to his brother's care. He cuddled him, held his bottle, changed him, and made him laugh.

One morning, while it was still dark outside, Jarvis heard screaming from the bedroom where the twins slept, and he ran in. Otis was standing over the twins' crib. Jarvis went to the crib and saw that Carl wasn't moving. He tickled his feet; Carl usually laughed when he did that.

"He's dead," Otis said.

Charlene ran into the room, looked into Jarvis's face, and shrieked at him, "You're in a world of trouble now!"

Jarvis tried to push the memory away, but he couldn't. Terrified, he opened his eyes.

Jarvis told Lisa about the experience in a letter: "Meditating used to make me calm down. It got me through the night. But it's been making me feel worse, bringing up all this shit—these terrible memories I want to forget. It's not what I need. It's too much."

Jarvis's letter prompted Lisa to bring a picture to her next visit, which she held up to the glass. The image showed a Buddha armed with weapons, including a flaming sword. She called it "wrathful Mañjuśrī." Jarvis said, "Now, that's a Buddha who might survive in San Quentin."

Jarvis asked Lisa what the weapons were for; wasn't this Buddhist thing all about peace, not fighting? She explained that the swords weren't for attacking external enemies but rather those inside us. They appear to represent violence, but their purpose is actually to "cut through ignorance and shields we build up over the course of our lives." She assured him that the image of Mañjuśrī could help him face the scariest memories that arose when he meditated. "I understand the desire to stop," she said, "but the pain you're feeling is a good thing."

He shook his head. "It doesn't feel good."

She responded, "But it will free you."

The next time he meditated, he imagined the warrior's sword in his hand as he searched for the memory of Carl. He quickly found where it was hidden inside a crystalized cocoon. Jarvis's body stiffened. He took the sword and used it to hack into the cocoon. His brother was inside. His baby brother. Carl! Jarvis began sobbing.

Without Jarvis's realizing it, Lisa and Chagdud Tulku were drawing him deeper into Buddhism. Over the past two years, Jarvis had been absorbing the religion's precepts and integrating its practices into his daily routine. As hard as it sometimes was, meditation had become the center of his life. He embraced concepts like Mañjuśrī that not long before he would have rejected as nuts.

Over the months that followed, Chagdud Tulku added yoga, prostrations, and mantras to Jarvis's practice. Lisa taught him basic yoga postures and then taught him mantras, which she described as strings of syllables to repeat while he meditated. "The repetition of sacred syllables purifies patterns of thought and speech," she said. "Repeat them and return to their safety when your mind wanders."

She also explained prostrations. "When we place our folded hands to our crown, we're honoring the qualities of enlightened form, embodied in the objects of our faith," she said, demonstrating. "We move them to our throat, where we're honoring the qualities of enlightened speech, and then to our heart, where we honor the qualities of enlightened mind." In the visiting booth she couldn't get onto the floor to show the prostration itself but explained, "When we touch our forehead, palms and knees to the floor, we're purifying our five poisons: ignorance, attachment, aversion, pride, and jealousy. Then we stand up into the freed poisons arising as wisdom."

Once again, Jarvis recoiled. *"Freed poisons arising as wisdom"? "Honoring the qualities of enlightened form"? And now they want me to bow?*

Lisa recognized his consternation, and she addressed it gently: "Of course, all these ideas and practices are foreign to you. All you have to do is consider them. If a Buddhist idea strikes you as interesting, contemplate it and meditate on it. Some practices may not make sense, but try them anyway and see what happens. One of the key Buddhist teachings is that you don't take anything as gospel just because someone told you. Try it out, and see if it's true for you."

She acknowledged that rituals, parables, and symbolism in Buddhism—touching your throat, repeating syllables in a language you don't understand, imagining a Buddha with a fiery sword—seem puzzling and possibly silly, but they share a purpose: to help us break free of lifelong patterns in our thinking that cause our suffering. They help us understand more about ourselves and the nature of existence. And they help us suffer less by revealing our purpose. They open our hearts and ultimately lead to enlightenment. She reminded him not to take her word for any of this but asked him to at least try it and see for himself.

At first, even one prostration was physically difficult, but the more he did, the more natural they became. He began integrating them into his daily practice and found they actually did what Lisa said they would do: "purify and prepare" him for meditation. When he preceded meditation with prostrations and repeated mantras, time and space disappeared. *He* disappeared.

Jarvis practiced with a dedication Lisa had rarely seen in other practitioners. She was impressed that he practiced with sincerity and bravery, continuing even when he panicked and wanted to stop. His insights impressed her. Once Jarvis said, "People always talk about their perfect meditation cushions, and sometimes I think it would be nice to have one, but maybe people without a cushion are luckier."

She asked him to explain.

"I've never had a cushion in my life," he said. "I've been on the cold, hard floor. It's not comfortable, but it's like the lady in the story, the one who knocked on a thousand doors. One hundred fifty years of pain in San Quentin has been absorbed into these floors. You talk about experiencing the suffering of all people. This is where it is, and I feel it *all*."

Lisa marveled at how far Jarvis had come in such a short time, and she told Chagdud Tulku about his latest revelations. The lama told Lisa he'd been thinking he wanted to meet Jarvis in person and asked if he could visit.

Lisa made arrangements and brought Rinpoche to San Quentin on a cold, gray winter morning. They joined a couple dozen men, women, and children who were gathered at the East Gate. A child tugged on his mother's coat and pointed at the man with long silver hair in a topknot and a silver beard, wearing scarlet robes over a crimson silk shirt, a floor-length burgundy skirt, and leather sandals.

After an hour, a guard instructed the visitors to line up and check in. Chagdud Tulku was told to remove his sandals, robe, and beads, and he was searched. Then Lisa guided him to the death row visiting hall, where they were escorted to chairs that faced a thick Plexiglas window. Jarvis was waiting on the other side.

Jarvis had been nervous, but when he saw the lama's face his apprehension faded, and he was comforted by the serenity that emanated from the teacher's eyes.

With Lisa translating, they exchanged greetings. "Looking through the glass is like watching you on a TV set," Chagdud Tulku said, and he broke into a wide grin.

"I can't believe you're really here," Jarvis said.

After some small talk, Chagdud Tulku asked, "Why do we sit with a glass wall between us but those down the hall are together in cages?"

Jarvis explained, "Some of these guys are allowed contact visits, and they can be with their families, but not me—not us in the hole."

Chagdud Tulku's eyebrows rose, and he repeated, *"The hole?"*

Jarvis said, "Solitary. We call it the hole."

The lama said, "I know the hole."

"What do you mean?" Jarvis asked. "You know the hole?"

"I was a young man when the Chinese occupied Tibet," the lama said. "Many Tibetan prisoners were put in stocks and publicly shamed. Some were beaten, and some were made to dig holes in the ground and forced to climb in. The hole was their prison. They dug the hole, and they lived in it. When they died, they were buried in the hole."

Jarvis thought, *This cat understands the hole.*

"I was fortunate and escaped," Chagdud Tulku continued, "though many others were killed. Twenty-three of my family died during those times. Only three survived." The teacher paused and then said, "The suffering was great."

He seemed to travel back to Tibet in his mind. "We were being chased, so we moved every night. It was winter, and the mountains were frozen. We hid in one lair after another. We did this for more than one year."

Jarvis was riveted.

The teacher said, "We survived by study, prayer, and meditation."

Lisa explained that Rinpoche escaped at the same time as the Dalai Lama and a hundred thousand other Tibetans. After that, Rinpoche helped develop Tibetan refugee communities in India and Nepal and then came to the United States, where he established centers for the study and practice of Tibetan Buddhism in North and South America, Europe, and Australia.

"And death row," Jarvis added.

When Lisa translated, the teacher beamed. "And death row."

They talked for an hour, and then a guard announced that visiting time was over. The lama spoke again. "You may not understand now, but it is your karma to be here," he said. "I said you are fortunate. As hard as it is to accept, this is where you have to be now. You may not see it, but you are fortunate to be in a place where you can know humanity's suffering and learn to see the perfection of all beings and yourself. Learn to see their perfection."

As the guard unlocked the door, Lisa spoke again: "Rinpoche reminds you to meditate every day. In your situation it will help you more than anything else."

When the teacher recognized that Jarvis was overwhelmed, Chagdud Tulku said, and Lisa translated, "His Eminence says, 'I am offering you many new ideas, so when I explain things to you, you may not understand at first. Don't be frustrated. It will become clear. Practice and open your heart, and your mind will follow.'"

Finally, the teacher said, "We leave you now. Remember this: we'll help you. You're in our prayers always. We'll always think of you."

The last thing he heard was Lisa: "Rinpoche says that he will see you soon now that he's your teacher and you are his student."

That was what Jarvis was left with as he was escorted back to the tier: *I am his student, and he is my teacher.*

That night in his cell, Jarvis tried to remember Rinpoche's words. There was a lot he didn't understand, but the lama said it was all right not to grasp the teachings all at once. He said, "Practice and open your heart, and your mind will follow."

"Your mind will follow."

Jarvis repeated those words, and they triggered a memory from his youth. He was nine when Mamie Procks grew ill. One evening she and Dennis sat him down and told him they couldn't take care of him anymore. Mamie held him close while he cried, but he pushed her away. He'd found safety and love and once again was being rejected.

After that Jarvis was placed in nine foster homes and three boys' homes, including some in which he was starved, beaten, and kept in squalor. At thirteen, he was moved from the foster care system into the division of juvenile justice, where the brutal treatment escalated. When he was arrested for petty crimes—stealing a bicycle, joyriding—he was placed in youth detention centers, where he was subjected to more beatings, burned, locked in closets, and made to pummel other boys. If he refused, counselors beat him harder. He ran away when he could and often found his way back to Harbor City, where he sometimes stayed with his aunt, Cynthia's sister Barbaree. There was always music playing. Barbaree played the same records over and over: Smokey Robinson, Gladys Knight, the Delfonics. She loved a song by George Clinton's Funkadelic, "Free Your Mind and Your Ass Will Follow," and must have played it a thousand times.

Jarvis laughed to himself at the thought of who had helped him understand the words of a great lama from Tibet. George Clinton. He said it aloud: "Free your mind and your ass will follow."

6

TAKING REFUGE

One day Lisa began their visit by saying, "Rinpoche has witnessed your sincerity and commitment to practice and plans to return to San Quentin to perform an 'empowerment' ceremony." She described the ceremony at which Jarvis would take refuge in the peace and safety of the Buddha, the dharma, and the sangha—the Three Jewels of Buddhism. She explained them. Buddha was the first jewel. Jarvis held on to Melody's explanation of the Buddha as "an ideal, what we aspire to be." He understood dharma as studying the Buddha's teachings and got that "study" wasn't simply learning the history, text, and concepts of Buddhism but incorporating them into your life. And the sangha was the community of people with you on the Buddhist path.

By taking those vows, Jarvis would formally become a Buddhist. Lisa asked, "What do you think?"

Jarvis hesitated. He'd been practicing a ragged form of the religion and benefiting immeasurably from it. It had made him rethink pretty much everything he thought he knew. The practice had been the hardest thing he'd ever done, but he sensed that Lisa was right when she said it could save him. Still, he didn't know if he wanted to become a Buddhist. What would it mean?

Lisa said he should take his time to decide—meditate on the question.

When Jarvis told Melody about Chagdud Tulku's offer, he admitted he wasn't sure what he should do.

"What worries you?" she asked.

"I don't join clubs," he said. "I'm not going to give myself over to *anything*. Every time I have, it was a mistake."

After reflecting, he continued, "Maybe it's that I don't deserve it"—he looked up—"like I'm no Buddhist, I'm"—he paused again—"a *fake*." His tone was solemn.

As Melody looked on silently, Jarvis pondered his reluctance further. He came to an explanation more fundamental and scarier to admit to himself, let alone anyone else. He thought, *A Buddhist is supposed to work to end suffering, but what about the suffering I caused? Rinpoche doesn't understand how violent I've been.* That thought led to one even more piercing: *I don't want to disappoint him.* The teacher believed he was a good person with a gentle spirit, and Jarvis worried that Chagdud Tulku would look inside him and see the truth: that he was the person Judge Savitt had described, someone evil and irredeemable.

He spoke again. "I don't think I'm worthy."

Melody responded, "If you're not worthy, Jarvis, no revered Tibetan lama would be coming to see you and offering these vows. Just relax. Allow this good thing to happen."

Melody made a formal request to the warden's office to hold the ceremony in the death row chapel or another private room, but the request was denied, as was her request to allow Chagdud Tulku to bring into the prison the sacred objects with which he normally conducted the ceremony. Regardless, it went forward on a spring morning. Frigid wind blew in through the Golden Gate. Jarvis woke up early and meditated. Breakfast was delivered, but he didn't eat. Finally a pair of guards came to his cell, and one of them asked Jarvis if he was ready.

Jarvis didn't respond.

The other guard asked, "Do you have everything you need?"

A strange feeling surged through Jarvis's body. For some inexplicable reason, he imagined that the guards had come to lead him not to his Buddhist teacher but to his execution—as they would if it was his time to be marched to the gas chamber.

The first guard repeated, "Masters, I said, are you ready?"

Startlingly, the answer was clear to him. He was ready.

"Do you have everything you need?"

He did. And he went with the guards, sensing that he was walking to his death.

Then, when he was sitting across from Chagdud Tulku, Melody, and a translator named Tsering Everest, Jarvis realized that just as he'd imagined, he *had* walked to his death—the death of the person he'd been. He looked into his teacher's eyes as he picked up the phone.

The four exchanged greetings. Tsering Everest introduced herself and then asked, "Are you okay? Are you ready for this?"

The same questions. As he said he was, he had chills again, because he realized he really was ready, not just for the ceremony but for whatever would come next in his life.

With Tsering Everest translating, Chagdud Tulku explained, "Normally I would bless you with various ritual items, but it's okay that we can't touch. The power of the ceremony is in your hearing the words and speaking them."

Jarvis leaned closer, and Chagdud Tulku began. "Is your mind clear?"

Jarvis said it was.

Tsering Everest then explained, "The empowerment is the doorway to the Vajrayana"—the form of Tibetan Buddhism taught by the lama—"and the commitment is to help all beings awaken to their true nature."

Chagdud Tulku had Jarvis repeat Tibetan phrases and recitations. He talked about the universality of suffering and the way suffering joins all beings. He reminded Jarvis to help people as much as he could. He repeated an instruction that Lisa had offered at one of their earliest meetings: Jarvis should see the perfection of all beings.

As he was instructed, Jarvis repeated the teacher's words: "I take refuge in the Buddha." "I take refuge in the dharma." "I take refuge in the sangha." He repeated each vow three times. Chagdud Tulku explained that with each repetition he was opening himself up more and that the more he opened, the more he would trust the path he was embarking on—a path that would lead to peace, happiness, and, ultimately, enlightenment.

Chagdud Tulku then said he was bestowing on him the protection of a benevolent, all-loving manifestation of the Buddha called Red Tara, the "mother of liberation."

An image appeared in Jarvis's mind: a scarlet, witchlike goddess emanating fire.

"Study her," Chagdud Tulku said. "She made a commitment that upon her enlightenment she would always respond swiftly to the suffering of whoever calls her."

Chagdud Tulku gave Jarvis what Tsering Everest called the "Red Tara initiation," instructing him to chant a mantra, *Om tare tam soha*, and visualize Red Tara in front of and above him, sending rays of warm light. "When you feel afraid, remember that she is with you," the teacher said. "Recite this prayer and visualize the light like wisdom in the form of nectar blessing you and all beings."

Tsering Everest translated the prayer to Red Tara as "Tara, please be aware of me; remove the obstacles in my path and grant my aspirations."

When the ceremony ended, as the visitors rose to leave, Chagdud Tulku said, "Today, as you've made these promises, we on the Buddhist path together are joined. Red Tara is with you. When you become afraid, call her and let those thoughts go in the wind."

*　　*　　*

When he and Lisa met the following week, Jarvis reflected on the ceremony. He admitted he'd been mystified by a lot of it. "I mean, Red Tara? A goddess who'll protect me? In *here*?" He said he'd looked her up in a book, and Red Tara looked different than he'd imagined. She wore a gold crown, had a scarlet body, a halo, and wielded a bow. "No pretend goddess is going to protect me in here."

Mainly he focused on something Chagdud Tulku had said the previous week—something he'd said several times before, as far back as his first letter. He'd said that Jarvis was fortunate and death row was a gift. Jarvis had thought, *If he believes that, he's naive.* In truth, it still pissed him off.

"That's something I just don't get," he said. "Maybe he's trying to make me feel better about where I am, but how can he believe San Quentin is a gift?"

"Tell me, Jarvis," Lisa responded, "what would your life have been like if you'd never been sent to death row, never been charged with the murder? Think about it. What would have happened?"

Jarvis was quiet a moment as he pictured that alternate path. Finally he responded, "There's no doubt what would have happened: I would have stayed on the course I'd always been on. Violence. That's who I was."

Lisa had once likened his cell in San Quentin to a monk's cell in a state-sponsored retreat. She was joking, but he reflected on it again now. "It's true," he said. "It's been a place to contemplate and study, to sit with all these new ideas and turn them around in my head and practice integrating them into my life. I never would have done any of that. I wouldn't have looked at my past, that scary shit—I'd still be running from it."

Then he realized something even more startling. "You know," he said, "the truth is, the sentence saved my life. I'd be dead. Literally dead."

"Why would you be dead?" she asked.

"If I wasn't in that monk's cell all those years, I would have been on that same path, and it led to one place. I'd have been killed or"— he paused and rubbed his eyes—"or have killed someone. I couldn't have kept going if I did that."

Jarvis remembered how angry and violent he'd been. "I was cursing out cops. Cons. Fighting. If I didn't start this spiritual practice, I'd still be that person until I got out—if I survived that long. And odds were against that.

"Then? I would have gotten out—maybe twenty years later. I'd have gone home to Harbor City, done what I did—robbing, shooting, being shot at." He envisioned it. "Yeah, I would have been in a body bag or put someone in one.

"Finally, even if I survived that"—he saw it clearly—"I would have been the same person I was before: spiritually dead."

That last thought shook him up. He continued, "So, yeah, in that way the death penalty saved my life. And *gave* me my life. I guess that's what Rinpoche meant when he said I'm fortunate. Everything changed because of that charge."

He had another thought: "I never would have meditated. Never would have learned about Buddhism. Never. Never would have been interested. Never would have met Rinpoche. Melody. Kelly. I never would have met you."

Jarvis thought back to the most mystifying, extraordinary part of the day he became a Buddhist: the morning of the empowerment ceremony, when guards took him from his cell. He recounted it to Lisa: "So they were walking me down, and it felt as if they were taking me to something other than the ceremony. To be executed. That's what I felt. The cop asked if I was ready, and I knew . . . I knew I was. I was ready to die. Now, what was that? I think I understand now: the person I'd been was ready to die and did die that day.

"My old self died. The person who was desensitized, numb, dead." He looked upward. "And from that death . . . it's like I became someone new. I'm *becoming* someone new."

Lisa countered, "You're becoming who you really are. You're discovering your true nature."

By then Jarvis had learned that Buddhism was filled with paradoxes and contradictions that messed with his mind. Sometimes it seemed as if those paradoxes were beyond his comprehension, but the mind is much more capacious than we think. He reveled in a fresh paradox: the death sentence that could kill him had given him life.

One day Melody asked Jarvis if he was interested in trying to publish the story he'd written about the scarred bodies of the prisoners, and she noticed his eyes widen. He submitted it to a magazine she gave him called *Wingspan: Journal of the Male Spirit*, and he forgot about it until Melody brought him a copy several months later. When he saw his story in print—"Scars" by Jarvis Jay Masters—he stared at the page, and a fragile look of astonishment crossed his face. Melody also saw conflict in his eyes, the pitting of stoicism that masked trepidation and self-doubt against something new: pride.

Susan Moon, editor of *Turning Wheel*, a Buddhist journal, was a member of Melody's writers' group. Susan read "Scars" and others of Jarvis's stories and found his writing stark, vivid, and filled with remarkable and heartrending insights. She arranged to visit him.

"I feel like I'm meeting an old friend," she said when she was sitting across from him. "I feel like I know you from your stories."

They talked about writing and Buddhism, and they did variations of the writing exercises he'd done with Melody. On one visit, Jarvis showed Susan a story he'd written about another challenging experience he'd faced that year. A group of inmates on the tier had planned an attack on two guards who'd been harassing them. It would have been pointless or even dangerous for Jarvis to ask the men to back off, but he contrived a way for them to express their rage and avoid violence.

It was the Fourth of July, and guards were eager to get off early to celebrate. Jarvis proposed a time when everyone on the tier would stuff towels into their toilets and begin flushing, continuing until water spilled out of every cell and the tier was flooded. "We'll make them work mopping it up," Jarvis said. "They won't be able to leave early. Now that will piss the hell out of them." When the men heard Jarvis's plan, they laughed their asses off. It was a perfect way to fuck with the guards. They put their knives away. As planned, the men flooded the tier and the pissed-off guards were forced to stay late.

Jarvis and Susan worked on the story together. Jarvis was a natural storyteller, so Susan's suggestions involved mostly structure, grammar, and fleshing out the characters. She taught him to identify clichés and replace them with his unique voice. Susan published the story, "Fourth of July," in *Turning Wheel*, and readers flooded the magazine with letters.

Susan visited most weeks. She and Melody worked with Jarvis on more stories. Once he confided in Melody, "Men in here are forgotten. That's one of my biggest fears. These stories are proof that I've lived and am alive. I'm staying in the game." He added, "And maybe I've found something I'm good at—something other than robbing and fighting."

Susan taught Jarvis about haiku, and they wrote some together. He said he hated poetry, but that changed when she read to him from a collection of poets, including Maya Angelou, Langston Hughes, and Alice Walker. He experimented with the form, and one day he brought a poem for her to read.

At that time Jarvis had been perfecting a recipe for pruno, prison wine that inmates made from a slurry of fruit cocktail, sugar, and other ingredients fermented in a Ziploc bag. He thought about the strangeness of inmates making wine, trying to make life as bearable as possible—as *normal* as possible—while waiting to be executed. Bouncing back and forth between those two realities, he came up with the idea of interweaving the recipe for pruno and the judge's reading of his death sentence.

Take peeled oranges,

Jarvis Masters, it is the judgment and sentence of this court,

one 8 oz. bowl of fruit cocktail,

that the charged information was true,

squeeze the fruit into a small plastic bag,

and the jury having previously, on said date,

and put the juice along with the mash inside,

found that the penalty shall be death,

add 16 oz. of water and seal the bag tightly.

and this Court having, on August 20, 1991,

Place the bag into your sink,

denied your motion for a new trial,

and heat it with hot running water for 15 minutes.

it is the order of this Court that you suffer death,

Wrap towels around the bag to keep it warm for fermentation.

said penalty to be inflicted within the walls of San Quentin,

Stash the bag in your cell undisturbed for 48 hours.

at which place you shall be put to death,

When the time has elapsed,

in the manner prescribed by law,

add 40 to 60 cubes of white sugar,

the date later to be fixed by the Court in warrant of execution.

six teaspoons of ketchup,

You are remanded to the custody of the warden of San Quentin,

then heat again for 30 minutes,

to be held by him pending final

secure the bag as done before,

determination of your appeal.

then stash the bag undisturbed again for 72 hours.

It is so ordered.

Reheat daily for 15 minutes.

In witness whereof,

After 72 hours,

I have hereon set my hand as Judge of this Superior Court,

with a spoon, skim off the mash,

and I have caused the seal of this Court to be affixed thereto.

pour the remaining portion into two 18 oz. cups.

May God have mercy on your soul.

Jarvis submitted "Recipe for Prison Pruno" to the 1992 PEN Prison Writing Program's annual writing contest, and it won an award.

The contrasts in Jarvis's life were dizzying. He was basking in the glow of the PEN award one morning when a guard passing him on the tier suddenly slammed him into the wall. His body filled with heat and anger; it was all he could do to restrain himself from retaliating. Another morning, his meditation was interrupted by gunfire from the exercise yard.

But the worst was yet to come in April of the same year.

In California there'd been a moratorium on executions since 1972, when the state Supreme Court declared them unconstitutional, but the death penalty had been reinstated in 1977. There had been no executions since then, but one was scheduled for the twenty-first of the month. When the night arrived, Robert Alton Harris, who'd been convicted of kidnapping and murder, was executed in the gas chamber.

That night Jarvis fell into a tortured sleep and had a nightmare, which he described in a letter to Melody. He'd dreamed he was with friends on a boat in the middle of the ocean. "A crew prepared diving equipment for them to explore the sea. The diving bell was green and shaped like a capsule or a miniature submarine. It had two small windows on each side and one thick chamber door in front. I was the first to go inside. The heavy chamber door slammed shut. I heard the sound of the crane lifting the diving bell off the boat and the chain belt lowering it slowly onto the surface of the water. Out the porthole I saw millions of bubbles and fish. It dove deep and I had an image that I was swallowed into the throat of Mother Earth. Then I became frightened. No one heard me as I descended. I [called on] Buddha, Allah, Jesus, Jehovah, Krishna. Then I collapsed onto the floor, and began thrashing, suffocating, vomiting, my body jerking."

When Jarvis awoke from the dream, his breathing was shallow and quick. He'd never felt as disoriented and scared. In that petrified state, he did the only thing he knew to do to help himself: he moved from the bunk to the floor, sat with his legs crossed and spine straight, and began to meditate. He felt as if he were in a wrestling match with his mind, prying it away from the panic and bringing it safely back into his body. It took an hour for him to calm down.

When he told Lisa about the night of the execution, Jarvis said he finally understood the power of meditation. There wasn't much in his life he could control, but he recalled Melody once saying, "Jarvis, you can control your mind." He hadn't fully understood what that meant, but now he did. He *could* control his mind. He understood what Rinpoche had given him: a lifeline. He held on, and it got him through the ache and fear caused by Harris's death. But even meditation itself produced wildly varying results. Sometimes he arose from the lotus position feeling a kind of serenity he'd never known. Other times he emerged feeling fragile and tender. Still other times he became lost in dark caves and emerged feeling depleted, feverish, and scared.

Lisa had told him about the loss of ego as a goal of meditation, and he experienced that sometimes. Time disappeared. *He* disappeared. "Melody," he wrote one evening, "it was like I left San Quentin for a while. . . . I don't know if I can explain what happened, but I think I understand the power of these practices. I don't think too many prisoners would live under the boots of their misery if they knew that the amount of work is the same to make ourselves miserable or make ourselves strong. And when we do, we can free ourselves without leaving our cells."

7

THE ONLY WAY OUT

For Jarvis, inspiration was an unfamiliar sensation, but he continued to feel it when he wrote. It felt as if a dormant part of himself had awakened. He submitted more articles and stories that were published in the *Utne Reader* and journals about spirituality and masculinity. In 1995, he submitted "Scars" to an anthology of African American writers called *Brotherman: The Odyssey of Black Men in America*. When the book was published, the editor sent Jarvis a copy. He was astonished when he saw his story among the writings of Frederick Douglass, Henry Louis Gates Jr., Alex Haley, Cornel West, and Richard Wright.

On Lisa's next visit, she suggested that Jarvis collect his stories in a book. She helped him select and edit them in what became *Finding*

Freedom: Writings from Death Row, published in fall 1997 by Padma Publishing, a press founded by Chagdud Tulku. Melody wrote an introduction, and Rinpoche contributed an afterword. When the book was released, Lisa arranged readings by Danny Glover and Geronimo Pratt, and *Finding Freedom* circulated throughout the Buddhist community and spread from there. Jarvis's San Quentin mailing address was published on the flyleaf, and letters flooded in.

Buddhists and non-Buddhists alike wrote to commiserate, applaud his resilience, and acknowledge his transformation. Many of them shared their own stories. He was startled by the intimate details some revealed about abuse and other trauma, as well as addiction, grief, suicide attempts, mental illness, and many other struggles. Many of those who wrote remarked on "Scars" and described their own scars, both physical and emotional.

The book was read in high schools; teachers assigned it in their classes and sent him packets of letters from students who had been inspired by his words. Jarvis heard from gang members, ex–gang members, prisoners, ex-prisoners, and their families. He was unsure how to respond to any of them. He felt he had nothing to tell them, but Lisa said people wouldn't write if there wasn't anything he could offer. She told him not to feel as if he had to carry others on his shoulders but to recognize that he'd been looking for a way to help people and he'd been given one.

Jarvis replied to every letter. He thanked the authors for writing, shared more of his experiences, offered solace, and asked them about their lives. It was the beginning of many new correspondences, some of which continued for years. Several of his pen pals became friends.

*   *   *

Pema Chödrön was a Buddhist nun who, much like the Dalai Lama, taught the religion's principles and practices and gave comfort and inspiration to countless people around the world. She wrote best-selling books, lectured, and led meditation workshops and retreats.

After a lecture in Sonoma, California, a woman presented Pema with a copy of *Finding Freedom*. She found it remarkable that a prisoner on death row had written something so profound. She was particularly impressed by the author's description of his journey to Buddhism. Like Chagdud Tulku, she practiced Vajrayana Buddhism, and she appreciated the way Jarvis hadn't simply adopted that tradition but had adapted it to who and where he was.

Pema wrote to Jarvis, and they began communicating. His letters affirmed her first impressions of him. He described his Buddhist practice with earnestness. He had every reason to be bitter and angry, but he was positive and joyful. Indeed, his letters made her laugh.

On her first visit to death row, Pema, wearing the traditional collared saffron shirt under a floor-length maroon robe, was put in one of the tiny visiting booths. When Jarvis was seated on the other side of the scuffed glass partition, she beamed.

Pema was diminutive, with close-cropped brown hair and sea-blue eyes that exuded kindness. They sat looking at each other for a while, smiling in silence. When they started talking, it was as if they were old friends catching up. They shared stories about their lives and discussed world events, books, and even movie scripts that Jarvis had read (his friends sent him the scripts). Even more than she had in his letters, Pema perceived his thoughtfulness and cheerfulness, and she found him even funnier in person.

Jarvis was charmed by her, too. By then he'd learned that she was a famous teacher and writer, but the woman across from him was down to earth, self-effacing. Her voice was quiet and comforting—though she kept up with him when it came to jokes and laughter. He glimpsed an unlikely mischievous side when she told him about babysitting her rambunctious four-year-old granddaughter.

"I was getting so exasperated and frustrated that I lost my temper," she said. "Here I was, this Buddhist nun whose stock in trade is calmness and tolerance, put over the edge by a toddler. When I calmed down, I said, 'Listen, sweetheart, let's say this is just between you and me. I have a reputation to uphold.'"

Pema visited whenever she was in the Bay Area, and their relationship deepened over months and then years. Jarvis went from calling her "Ani Pema"* to his "dharma mom" to "Moms" to "Mama." The last was a word he used with humor, but it reflected his love for her.

Jarvis had a spiritual teacher in Chagdud Tulku, but Pema helped guide his practice. She instructed and encouraged him and sometimes gently admonished him.

Once he wrote her when he was feeling down. "I've been in a bad place," he admitted, "so I let my practice slide."

*"Ani" is the honorific for a Buddhist nun; it's the equivalent of calling her "Sister Pema."

Pema responded, "Maybe you didn't let your practice slide because you're in a bad place, but you're in a bad place because you let your practice slide."

She signed the postcard "Mom's here!" and drew a smiley face in purple ink.

Jarvis once asked about the name she'd had before she became Pema Chödrön, and he had to laugh when she said she used to be Deirdre Blomfield-Brown. When he stopped, he asked, *"Deirdre?"* He laughed harder. "So one day you wake up and say, 'I think I'm going to change my name. But not to, like, Sue or Patty.'"

She joined him laughing, and then she told a story that riveted him. "I was a good Catholic girl," she said. "I went to Miss Porter's School, which was a very fancy East Coast school for girls. Jackie Kennedy went there. Then UC Berkeley for college, where I got bachelor's and master's degrees, and then taught elementary school. I got married, divorced, and married again.

"I was married eight years, and then one day my husband came home and told me he was in love with someone else and was leaving me."

Jarvis couldn't imagine her in that situation. "Man, oh, man," he said. "That's terrible."

"I was devastated," she said. "It was so final. He didn't say 'Maybe' or 'Let's go to a counselor.' It was finished."

She continued, "I had these mean-hearted emotions, hatred of my husband and his girlfriend. I imagined burning their house

83

down. I'd always been this good girl, 'Miss Sunshine,' and I'm going '*Whoa* . . . I didn't even know I had this in me.'"

Jarvis laughed again. "I can't see you burning anyone's house down. That's something *I* might have done, but *you?*"

"I had to figure it out; I was in so much pain and so confused, so I went to therapy and even tried Scientology and primal-scream therapy—I ran from that when I heard this shrieking in the next room. I looked into Eastern mysticism and religions and tried meditation, but nothing helped."

She said, "I was thumbing through a magazine and came to an article called 'Working with Negativity' by a Tibetan Buddhist master, Chögyam Trungpa Rinpoche. Before that, I'd tried different kinds of meditation, and the teachers all talked about pushing negative feelings away—transcending them—and I thought, 'If I could do that, I gladly would, but I can't.'

"But this teacher's message was the opposite. He taught that people *shouldn't* try to leave behind or transcend whatever they struggled with, because pain, sadness, and despair—he called those emotions 'negativity'—are useful, and we can learn from them. He said people have to experience the bad feelings in order to heal.

"It was like he was speaking directly to me. He was saying there was nothing wrong with me for feeling so badly—that is, the negativity wasn't the problem. The problem was the way I spun off from the hurt and sadness."

Jarvis asked, "What do you mean 'spun off'?"

"Telling myself stories about what I'd done wrong, how I didn't know how I'd cope, envisioning my life without him. Imagining burning his house down was one, too."

She laughed quietly. "I recognized that it was easier to fantasize about revenge than it was to feel the pain of the loss and being rejected."

She explained that rather than spinning out stories that focused on questions such as "How could he do this to me?" "How will I survive without him?" "What was wrong with me that caused him to leave?" "How can I best torture him?"—she needed to stay with the hurt.

"So I read more about the teacher and Tibetan Buddhism, and eventually I went to Europe to study it. I did that for two years and then was ordained a novice nun. My teacher renamed me."

Pema Chödrön means "Lotus, Torch of the Dharma" or "Lamp of the Truth."

"So here's what it is," she said. "I'd attributed the pain I'd felt when my husband left to the loss, but I realized it was fear. I was unmoored—groundless—free-falling without a net. Groundlessness is what it is. Groundlessness is *terrifying*, but it's an opportunity."

Jarvis had been meditating for more than a decade. He'd practiced breathwork and mindfulness, and they'd helped him endure the stressful years of the trial and the penalty phase. They'd helped him stay sane and eased the panic he periodically felt.

The better he became at meditation, the more it helped him

face trauma he'd experienced and learn and explore. Sometimes terrible memories and fears—of execution, of guards—arose, but he used meditation to push them aside—to try to transcend the pain he'd carried with him his whole life. But now Pema challenged him to go back to the worst memories and fears again—to intentionally meditate on them. She said *not* to push them away, *not* to try to transcend them, *not* to run from them, but to *go toward* them.

Jarvis said, "You've got to be kidding."

"It isn't a onetime thing," Pema said. "It's a process. We chip away a piece at a time. To free ourselves, we have to keep going, to go deeper."

Jarvis felt weary and afraid. "Deeper?" He shook his head. "That is not something I want to do."

"I know," she said. Then she counseled, "It feels like going back to the pain will kill you, but it won't. The thing is, yes, the pain hurts, but only by facing it will it stop chasing you. The thoughts will come, they're very strong, and you sit with them. You experience the sharp feelings and stay there.

"People think as a Buddhist you want to transcend the everyday, transcend the past, transcend the pain. But the goal isn't dangling above the messiness of life, it's sitting in it; you don't want to transcend the past but be there fully. When you fully connect with your past . . . that's when it begins to lose its ability to harm you—to control you. What you do is go to the events; you don't judge them as good or bad, and you sit with them even if they scare you." She added, "*Especially* if they scare you."

She offered a poignant example: "Let's say your child is very ill. All you want to do is run away from the bad feelings. It feels as if they will kill you—that's how afraid you are. You do anything not to feel them. But unless you feel them, they don't go away. And here's the thing: if you sit with those feelings, it doesn't feel good, but it feels honest and true. When you stop running, you can be *with* your child who's ill, which is where you want to be for yourself and for him."

Pema evoked an experience that had haunted Jarvis since he was little: the death of his baby brother. "It was too much to feel the pain of Carl's death," she said, "so you ran from it by spinning out stories. It's natural."

"Stories? What stories?"

"One of the stories was about Otis, that he might have been involved in Carl's death. If he was, something sinister had happened, and you and your siblings might be in peril. If that were true, you were living with the person who killed your little brother! That was a terrifying story. You'd left the experience itself the moment you saw that Carl was dead. You left again in the story that it was your fault Carl died because you'd failed to protect him.

"You've lived with that story about your responsibility for Carl's death your whole life, and that one led to other stories—ones that shaped the way you think about yourself and the choices you've made. If you caused your brother to die, you must be a terrible person. Your actions affirmed that. Twenty years later you're in San Quentin, and you're charged with murdering a guard. You didn't kill anyone, but maybe you felt as if you had. You felt as if you'd killed Carl. A part of you—a very deep part of you—still feels, 'No wonder I'm on death row. The judge was right. I deserve to be here.'"

Pema stopped and let Jarvis absorb her words. He was holding back tears.

"Go back and meditate on the experience. It's scary, and you think you can't survive if you go there. But there's always a break in the stories we tell ourselves. It's just the way our minds work. There's a pause. At that point it's like waking up from a dream, and you remember what you're doing. That's the opportunity. You can learn to recognize the pause. You think, *I'm in the story again.* That's when you have the opportunity to leave the story and go back to your breath.

"So you're meditating and you're home again with your mother and Otis. You run into the bedroom and see that Carl is dead. That's when you've always run from the immediate experience and the stories began. You spun off into the story about what Otis might have done or how you killed Carl—how it's your fault. You're in the story as you meditate, but it stops for a moment. It will—you'll see. That's when you can leave the story by taking a breath and returning to your body. Then you return to the experience—the most important moment—the moment you've spent your life avoiding."

"What moment?" Jarvis asked. He didn't want to hear the answer.

"When you ran in and saw Carl and realized he had died. That's the moment you glossed over because of how painful it was. You glossed over the heart of the experience."

"The *heart?*"

"The heart," she said. "You loved Carl. That's the heart. You loved him so much. And he was gone. That's the pain you have to face and finally feel. Go to your body and feel it there. Your body is always there for you. Your breath. Only when you feel it will you free yourself, and yes, the pain will be great."

Jarvis meditated that night and pictured Carl's face. After all those years, the image was still vivid: the baby's gentle smile and trusting eyes. Then he heard Otis's scream, and Jarvis tensed. He ran into the bedroom, looked into the crib, and saw Carl's lifeless body. Carl was dead.

As it had done so often before, Jarvis's mind started to retreat into the familiar stories—about Otis's involvement, his own complicity, and the trouble he'd get into. But then, as Pema promised, he sensed a pause. In that moment, he gained perspective. Inside the story, he was the young boy facing the horror for the first time, but the pause allowed him to recognize that he was now a grown man, decades away from that awful moment. Armed with that perspective, he could return to his body and the bedroom: the moment he saw Carl. He touched him, but the baby didn't move. His baby brother was dead. Little, innocent Carl. He loved him so much. He loved him more purely than he'd loved anyone.

He felt all the pain he couldn't face for all those years. And he felt a sense of release. Once he started sobbing, he couldn't stop.

Sometimes meditation still brought serenity and stillness, but sometimes other terrible memories came. Once, he returned to Harbor City, where he met up with his older brothers, Tommy and Robbie,

Cynthia's eldest children. They forced him to fight. A crowd would gather, people screaming "Kill him, kill him!" and Tommy and Robbie threw Jarvis into the center with some other boy. Jarvis fought ferociously, punching and kicking. He was made to fight the little brothers of Tommy's and Robbie's friends, and his brothers bet on him. If he lost, they kicked the shit out of him. He felt bad beating those kids; they hadn't done anything to him. The guilt, the punches, the fury—hatred of his brothers.

Another time—he was sixteen—Jarvis was hanging out with a boy with whom he'd escaped a lockup. His friend had stolen drugs from a street gang. They were at a party, and Jarvis looked outside and saw members of the gang waiting for them in a car. High on weed and booze and armed with pistols, they ran out the front door and blindly opened fire. The car sped away, and their bullets sprayed the house across the street. Later he learned that a family had been in the house, and the parents grabbed their children, fell to the floor, and held on to them, scared to death.

While he meditated, the scene replayed in Jarvis's head, not from his vantage point outside, shooting, but from the perspective of the family. He began to flee the memory, to enter the story of what followed—the APB, the police. Then the pause came, and he breathed. He made himself return, and he became the terrified parents holding their children. He began quaking. He felt their terror.

"I need to apologize," Jarvis told Pema one day, "to all these people. I need to tell them I'm sorry."

He recalled one of Chagdud Tulku's instructions at the empowerment ceremony: he should confess his mistakes and ask for forgiveness. But to whom? In Christianity, absolution comes from confession and contrition. Jarvis felt that was too easy. A priest could forgive you, but you hadn't harmed the priest.

"I feel like I have to apologize to those people, but I can't," he said. "I don't even know their names."

Ani Pema counseled, "When you meditate, find the mother and father and their babies. Think of the people in the stores you robbed, the boys you fought. Find them in your mind, and don't run from them. Acknowledge them. Acknowledge what you did. Don't dismiss them or minimize the hurt you caused them. It doesn't help your victims or anyone else if guilt and shame drag you down. Instead, continue to leave behind your self-obsession and free yourself from your past and go forward. Continue facing your pain, because the more you free yourself from being held back by your past, the more you can focus on others. Let your experiences hurting people push you forward as you say to yourself, 'From now on, I'm going to spend my life helping people.' That, Jarvis, is your challenge now. That is your karma."

8

KARMA

When Pema spoke the word *karma*, it reverberated with Jarvis. He'd heard it from Rinpoche, who once said his karma was to be on death row. He heard it from Lisa—indeed, from every Buddhist he'd ever met or read.

He'd first noticed the word during the voir dire stage of his trial, when a potential juror claimed he was a Buddhist. When a lawyer asked if as a Buddhist he could vote for a death sentence, the man said he could. He believed in eye-for-an-eye justice and felt that sending a person to death could benefit them by balancing their "spiritual bank account"—that is, it could "fix their karma."

That statement had disgusted Jarvis. Kill someone if you want, but don't try to ease your conscience by saying it's for their own good.

Jarvis asked Pema if she believed in the idea of a spiritual bank account. Is that what karma is? If so, what was his karma? Would he have to die to pay his karmic debt even though he'd never killed anyone?

Then he asked her about the concept of karma itself. "So do all poor people have bad karma? Innocent victims of wars? Children born with terminal illnesses or their parents who have to watch them die? Is it their karma?"

Pema said, "That's not it. Karma isn't justice or fairness. No one deserves to be born into a violent home or with a terrible disease, but many people are. No parent deserves to watch a child die, but it happens all the time. You may be born with privilege, you may be born in poverty, you may be born healthy or sick. No, it's not fair, but fairness doesn't apply—*life* isn't fair.

"The parents didn't lose their child because of their karma," she said. "Their karma is the situation they're left with; it's their reality. How will they respond is the question. Any parent whose child dies would feel angry and bitter. For some, that's it—they're bitter and angry for the rest of their lives. It's understandable. But there are other options. Some parents find relief by appreciating the time they had with their child, holding their son or daughter in their hearts, recalling the love they shared. Some devote their lives to helping other grieving parents."

Pema explained that ultimately what was relevant in Jarvis's life wasn't how he got to San Quentin or death row. His karma was simply the fact that he was there. What mattered was what he would do while there. Many people on death row are drawn into bitterness, vengeance, and rage and many into madness. Jarvis had chosen a different path: Buddhism and all it entails. She explained that karma boils down to one relevant fact and one vital question. The fact: "This is where I am today." The question: "How will I use it?"

Jarvis was more committed than ever to making the most of his time—as much as he could, staying focused on what Pema had described as his San Quentin karma. He practiced with more dedication than ever. He awoke between four and five every morning and did prostrations for a half hour and then yoga for an hour. Afterward, he meditated for two hours or more, running a mala through his fingers. Many Buddhists use malas, small strings of wooden prayer beads, when they meditate. Jarvis wasn't allowed to have an actual mala, so he made his own by poking holes in aspirin tablets and stringing them onto a thread he'd pulled from a sock.

Jarvis read more books about Buddhism; he was interested in the history of the religion, including the investigations into the historical Buddha. Throughout the day and evening, he made an effort to connect with as many prisoners on the tier as possible, though he was limited to conversations with inmates nearby. He had the opportunity to spend time with more inmates on the yard. When he went out, he played basketball and talked with other men. He approached inmates who seemed isolated or troubled and gently tried to engage them. He recalled the men he had written about in "Scars." Like them, some rebuffed him, some angrily, but others seemed happy to talk to someone interested in hearing about their lives. Men sometimes asked about "this Buddhist thing you're into." Rather than trying to explain the religion, Jarvis described meditation and told Buddhist stories.

In the evenings there was dinner, maybe chess, listening to music or the news, watching TV, and more writing. Using a fishline made of thread from bedsheets, a con down the tier passed Jarvis tightly folded letters. The inmate couldn't read, so before Jarvis began his nightly meditation, he read the letters aloud, projecting his voice as far as he could. The man and other inmates nearby listened raptly as Jarvis read letters from the prisoner's mother, whose loving words lulled the tier to sleep.

With his deepening connections with prisoners and friends and a full schedule each day, Jarvis was feeling as content as he'd ever been. His life was full and rich, but then, on November 17, 2002, he received devastating news. Chagdud Tulku Rinpoche had been ill. On his most recent visit to San Quentin, he had been too frail to get out of a wheelchair. Nevertheless it was a shock when Lisa said their teacher had died.

Some of Chagdud Tulku's students celebrated the circumstances of his "physical death." They claimed that he'd continued to sit in meditation for five days after he stopped breathing; his body hadn't deteriorated. They said the teacher had been freed of his human form and attained enlightenment.

Jarvis didn't know about that. He only knew that his heart was broken.

Jarvis recalled his first letter to Rinpoche twelve years before and the teacher's response, which arrived the evening after he'd been sentenced to death. It felt like a minute ago and a lifetime ago. Since then, Rinpoche had encouraged him, reassured him, and given him his vows—that is, he made him a Buddhist. He had taught him well. Jarvis grasped how well when he was on the yard one day and an inmate who'd heard about his conversion asked, "How can you be a Buddhist in this shithole?"

Without thinking, Jarvis responded, "The question for me is 'How can you be in this shithole without being a Buddhist?'"

He imagined Rinpoche smiling at the thought that Jarvis was learning to think like him. Another time he recognized Chagdud Tulku's influence was the day the lama called him a bodhisattva, defining it as a person who devotes his life to preventing suffering and benefiting others. Jarvis flinched when he heard it. He argued, "I'm the *opposite* of a bodhisattva. I didn't prevent suffering; I caused it." He added, "What have I ever done to help anyone?"

The lama said he was asking the wrong question. Jarvis waited for Rinpoche to tell him what the right question was, but the lama just shrugged.

The right question came to him that night when he pondered the teacher's meaning. The question wasn't what he'd done to help others, but what he would do now.

When he realized he knew the answer himself, Jarvis imagined Chagdud Tulku smiling again. And Jarvis smiled, too, as he understood that the lama would live inside him forever.

Rinpoche led Jarvis forward in other ways. He'd given him

permission to take from Buddhism what helped him and reject his own and others' preconceptions about what a Buddhist should be. He showed Jarvis that Buddhism is replete with paradoxes and contradictions because life itself is. And he pointed him toward the central paradox of the faith: that the more one accepts suffering, the less one suffers.

The more Jarvis thought about his teacher, the more he understood that Chagdud Tulku's students were right. There *was* something to celebrate: their teacher's life and the lessons that had changed him. We're all doing time. We're all in prison. We're all on death row. And we can all free ourselves.

Before he died, Chagdud Tulku ordained a number of students as lamas. Lisa was one of them. He gave her the name Lama Shenpen Drolma—*shenpen* means "to benefit others," and "Drolma" is the Tibetan equivalent of Tara, the "mother of liberation," which Rinpoche "gave" Jarvis. Three years later Lama Shenpen established a retreat center in southern New Mexico. Since then she'd been in the Bay Area less often. She and Jarvis remained in touch, but with her away and Chagdud Tulku gone, Pema became his main teacher. There was no official passing of the torch, and nothing dramatically changed in their relationship; they'd already been studying dharma together, and she had already been guiding his practice. Their teacher-pupil relationship fit comfortably inside their friendship.

They studied Buddhist concepts that were new to him, and they returned to ones he'd learned about before, such as karma and the

Four Noble Truths. Jarvis had often heard about the Three Jewels. Back when Rinpoche conducted the empowerment ceremony, he had Jarvis take refuge in them. For Jarvis, the first and second jewels, the Buddha and dharma—the Buddha himself and his teachings— seemed straightforward, at least as straightforward as anything in Buddhism is. Jarvis hadn't thought much about the third jewel, the sangha, but Pema explained it as those together on the Buddhist journey, including nuns, monks, teachers, and practitioners, as well as one's immediate circle of people "who share their experiences, study together, teach each other, and are on the same path."

Jarvis interjected, "Like a gang."

The word *gang* just popped out, and it jarred him.

Pema was surprised too, and she asked him what he meant.

"Well, that's what a gang is," Jarvis said thoughtfully. "People on the same path. Learning, teaching, studying the same books, living the same code." He concluded, "I guess the gang was my sangha back then."

"I guess it *was* your sangha," she agreed.

"A reflection of who I was then—who we all were," he continued. "We were on a path together."

"Tell me about the path."

"It was a path of violence. If you showed any sign of weakness, you were in trouble. Learning together? What we learned was not to feel." He paused, took a deep breath, and said, "I guess I was born into that sangha—a sangha with all the kids in our neighborhood together on the path, and that path led to prison. On that path we were beaten and then told, 'If you cry, you'll get it twice as hard.' 'Do not fight, but if you fight, you had better beat the son of a bitch. If you lose don't bother coming home.' Running from punishment, you got it worse. I learned to never back down, even if I knew I'd get beat. *Especially* if I knew I'd get beat. Boys—even teachers, counselors—knew not to mess with me. If they didn't, they learned pretty quick."

Jarvis reflected back to a time he had gone home to Harbor City after escaping from a California Youth Authority lockup. His brother Tommy said he could stay with him if he worked in his heroin business, standing guard with a shotgun during deals. "He said, 'You won't have to shoot anyone, just show the gun,' and I didn't want to, but Tommy said, 'What's wrong with you? I'm trying to hook you up. YA made you a pussy.' I gave in. I didn't want to disappoint Tommy, but the main reason I gave in: I was going to show him I *wasn't* a pussy. A pussy was the worst thing you could be. *That's* the path we were all on together.

"Then in San Quentin, our teachers were the revolutionaries, our practice was obedience, intimidation, and violence. It was about sacrifice: sacrificing our *selves* and, if necessary, our lives. The sangha was the soldiers who trained together."

They sat for a while, until Pema broke the silence. "You have a different sangha now," she said. "I think of it as people who are evolving, searching, kind, respectful, sensitive, supportive, and loving."

Jarvis nodded. The truth of that sank in. He *did* have a sangha—a true sangha now. It had begun with Melody and grown to include more than two dozen friends and fellow practitioners helping one another, devoted to one another.

*   *   *

Indeed, Jarvis's sangha had grown organically and continued to expand as members brought in others. Not long after Chagdud Tulku's death, Pema told a friend, Pamela Krasney, about Jarvis and encouraged her to visit. When she did, Pamela, an advocate for prison reform and other social justice causes, marveled that she felt an instant and deep connection with a person on death row. And Jarvis felt immediately connected to Pamela. He noticed that she seemed more alive than anyone he'd ever met.

Soon Pamela became one of his most committed supporters and closest friends. She brought her husband, Marty, and their children, Samantha and Parker, to visit. They all exchanged letters and sent postcards of their travels, and joined the Jarvistas, a growing group of Jarvis's supporters working for his exoneration.

Pamela became Jarvis's fiercest advocate. She would storm into the office of Jarvis's appellate attorneys, offer (unsolicited) advice about the appeal, and push them to get the state court to expedite Jarvis's case. Once, Pamela told Melody she'd used her connections to get Judge Savitt's home number and was going to call and confront her about Jarvis's sentence. When Melody heard the plan, she was appalled and said, "You can't call up a judge like she's a socialite to talk over a capital case," but Pamela ignored her. Savitt answered the phone and rebuked Pamela for calling, but Pamela ignored the reproach and asked the judge to lunch. (Savitt declined.)

Pamela wrote several hundred letters on Jarvis's behalf. She and Marty funded his canteen account so he could buy chips and candy bars through the commissary and sent him a TV and books. Jarvis was partial to histories of world wars and biographies of presidents, inventors, and civil rights leaders. When he expressed an interest in astronomy, Pamela sent books and a star chart, which he taped on his cell wall using the adhesive edges from sheets of postage stamps. He studied the phases of the moon and calculated when the next eclipse would be visible at a time when he could be on the yard.

When the day came, Jarvis went out and unfolded the chart on the ground. He looked up at the cloudless sky, and there it was.

In a letter thanking Pamela for the chart, Jarvis wrote, "People on the yard saw what I was doing, and they looked up, too. They passed the chart around and asked questions. I looked around and saw men from one side of the yard to the other all looking up to the sky. One of the rarest spectacles I've ever seen. Then I look over at the guards in the gun towers—they were looking up, too. Everyone just looking into the sky."

He continued, "Everyone was just gazing up, staring at this moon. Then the moon started slipping away and was gone just like that. The yard was never quiet, but there was only silence."

Marie Williams* attended a Buddhist retreat at a meditation center in Sonoma County, at which an instructor recommended the book *Finding Freedom*. Williams bought it and was transfixed by the author's

---

*Citing privacy concerns, "Marie Williams" spoke under the condition that I refer to her with a pseudonym and change details that could identify her or her family.

story of transformation. This man spent most of his life in prison, and he had every reason to be bitter, hard, and vengeful. But he seemed to be optimistic and joyful.

Marie wrote Jarvis, and the two began corresponding. Jarvis wanted to hear all about her life in San Francisco, and she wanted to know all she could about Jarvis—about his family, his childhood, and experiences in prison—simple things: what he ate, how he spent his time, what his cell was like, which he described as a dorm room at a university he'd never applied to.

After a year of letters, which came with increasing frequency, Marie asked if he'd like her to visit. She filled out the necessary forms, and after she was approved she came to San Quentin.

Marie had never been to a prison and was nervous when she checked in, passed through security, and entered the visiting hall. A guard guided her to a chair that faced a small room on the other side of a window where Jarvis was waiting.

After knowing each other only through letters, their first face-to-face meeting was awkward. They sized each other up through the Plexiglas, and, after a moment, they both smiled. Jarvis broke the ice with small talk. She'd written him about her family but he wanted to know more. They talked about religion. Marie said she'd been raised Catholic but had become disillusioned with the religion, and a divorce ended her remaining attachment to the church. She wasn't a Buddhist but described her spirituality as a blend of Eastern and Western religions and humanism. She benefited from meditating, which was why she'd attended the retreat where she'd first heard about his book.

Jarvis was an animated storyteller, and his laughter was infectious. He talked about who he had been before he became a Buddhist. "If you saw me walking toward you back then, you would have crossed the street and been smart to." He told her about his journey to Buddhism.

Midway through the visit, Marie no longer felt nervous; she'd forgotten she was in a prison. She and Jarvis talked for two hours before a guard ended the meeting.

Jarvis and Marie exchanged more letters, which over time became longer, newsier, and more personal, and she visited again. He introduced her to Pamela, and the two had lunch. Marie expressed interest in learning more about Jarvis's case, so Pamela gave her shopping bags full of documents. The more Marie read, the more she was convinced that he was innocent. The injustice of his conviction and sentence enraged her. She began attending meetings of the Jarvistas, and she volunteered to help in their campaign to free him.

A year went by. Marie visited more frequently. Sometimes when she left San Quentin and encountered the clean air and blue sky, she imagined the hellish cell he was returning to, and she cried. It was inconceivable to her that this fiercely intelligent, sensitive man had spent his life locked in cages. But then she thought about the contrast between the environment in which he lived and his positivity, lightheartedness, and thoughtfulness, and her sadness became a kind of amazement. In truth, he was more positive and joyful than many people she knew on the outside.

Marie imagined what it might be like if he weren't in prison and they could get to know each other under normal circumstances.

Jarvis thought about Marie, too, though he reined in his growing affection for her. He cherished her friendship and didn't want to chase her away by expressing his feelings. But his changing feelings found their way into his letters, which became more intimate. He saw that her feelings were changing, too, when in her letters she referred to their "heart connection."

KILL THE BUDDHA

Through his decades in San Quentin in the AC and other cell-blocks, Jarvis was often moved randomly from one cell and tier to another. There'd be no warning. A guard would show up and tell him to get up, he was moving. If he was lucky, he'd be allowed to grab his few possessions.

Over those years he was housed alongside some of the most notorious inmates on death row, including, for a year, Charles Manson.

Back in the mid-1990s, Jarvis was moved to a new Adjustment Center cell and heard a voice. "Welcome, brother."

His new neighbor was Stanley "Tookie" Williams, a cofounder of the Crips, one of America's most notorious street gangs. The year

107

Jarvis arrived in San Quentin, Williams had been convicted of four counts of homicide and sentenced to death.

Jarvis and Tookie had grown up fewer than twenty miles from each other—Tookie in South-Central LA, Jarvis in Harbor City, neighborhoods steeped in poverty and violence. Though their backgrounds were similar, they were unlike each other in appearance and manner. A decade younger than Tookie, Jarvis was just over six feet tall, lean, and clean-shaven, with close-shaved hair. Tookie was shorter but with a weightlifter's bulk. He wore his hair in long braids. Jarvis could be boisterous and teasing, but he was generally reserved; Tookie was fierce, bombastic, and volatile.

During the months they were death row neighbors, they talked about their families in Southern California and their experiences in juvenile jails. They also talked about writing. Like Jarvis, Tookie had published articles and books, including a memoir, and he was working on a children's book to educate young people about drugs and gangs. They read each other's stories and offered criticism and suggestions.

Belying his tough facade and reputation, Tookie was warm and open. Jarvis respected Tookie's efforts to mitigate the harm he'd caused by renouncing the Crips, brokering a peace treaty between the rival Crips and Bloods.

They were separated three months later when Jarvis was moved again, this time to another tier, and he didn't see Tookie for a decade. He'd heard reports, though, including, in fall 2005, that Williams's appeals were finally exhausted and his execution date had been set. In early December, Jarvis saw his old friend one last time. Both men were in the visiting hall. Williams was meeting his lawyers, discussing last-minute strategies to save his life. Jarvis yelled out, "Hey, man, how you doing?" Tookie responded, "Left Hand!"—inmates called Jarvis "Left" or "Left Hand" because he was a southpaw—"It's been a long time, brother!" Jarvis asked Tookie how he was holding up— "You're in my thoughts, man"—and Tookie assured him that the execution wasn't going to happen—his lawyers would stop it.

But four days later, on December 13, 2005, Jarvis heard that the execution was scheduled for midnight.

That night there was an ominous pall on death row. Helicopters could be heard overhead. Protesters gathered outside San Quentin, mostly Williams's supporters and opponents of the death penalty. Jesse Jackson and Joan Baez were there. Baez sang "Swing Low, Sweet Chariot."

On the tiers, some inmates tried to ignore the pending execution, but many listened to radio coverage of the doomed last-minute efforts to stop it. First the California Supreme Court refused to intervene. Then the US Supreme Court declined to hear the case. Governor Arnold Schwarzenegger—Tookie's last chance—denied clemency.

Less than an hour after midnight, the news of Tookie's execution reached death row.

When Jarvis saw Pema shortly afterward, he poured out his sorrow. He talked about other executions since he'd been on death row—six in all. Those deaths devastated Jarvis, but Tookie's felt different.

Jarvis said that many inmates spent the evening of the execution watching sports on TV and some made small talk, but their conversations were louder than usual, as if to drown out the event taking place a few hundred yards away. Jarvis wanted to escape, too, to join others and tune out what was happening, but he didn't—he couldn't. "It felt like my heart was being torn out," he said.

Then he said, "I thought this Buddhist shit was supposed to protect you."

Pema looked at him and sighed. "Jarvis," she said, "there's no protection from pain and grief. It's a fantasy to think we can be protected. You wouldn't want to not feel grief when someone dies. What kind of person would that make you? A very coldhearted person."

"It's easier to be a coldhearted person," he said.

"Yes, but would you ever want to be that unfeeling person again?"

Jarvis didn't answer for a minute. Finally, he whispered, "No."

Over the following months, as Jarvis mourned Tookie's death, his own sentence was also on his mind—as were his hopes for justice and exoneration.

When he was sentenced to death in 1990, there had been a five-year wait for the state to appoint a condemned inmate an appellate lawyer, so Jarvis asked Melody if she could find an attorney who would take his case immediately. She approached Joseph Baxter, a lawyer who was also a Buddhist.

Baxter went to see Jarvis later that year. He had unruly hair and blue-gray eyes, and he spoke with a slow, measured drawl. He wore a rumpled suit and pin-striped shirt, and in many ways he came across as the stereotypical southern lawyer despite the fact that he was from Brooklyn.

Baxter told Jarvis that he'd been reviewing the case and found it replete with violations of his rights; there were numerous grounds for an appeal. He said he'd take it on.

Jarvis was distrustful of lawyers. The good they'd done him was evidenced by his years in jails and prison, never mind his death sentence. However, he was grateful to have Baxter, who teamed up with another appellate lawyer, Richard Targow, and Scott Kauffman, an attorney with the California Appellate Project (CAP). In 2001, they filed a 515-page brief to begin the appeal of Jarvis's conviction. Four years later, in 2005, they also filed a habeas corpus petition.

There'd been no movement on the case until, on February 14, 2007—Valentine's Day—Jarvis received a message from Baxter, informing him that the California Supreme Court had responded to one of the filings with an "order to show cause." The Marin County court, where he'd been convicted, was required to hold a hearing and review his lawyers' claims that Jarvis's trial had been a travesty. Joe said the hearing could lead to a new trial or even his exoneration.

Marie visited that day and they were elated. It was the best Valentine's gift they could have received.

*   *   *

Back when Jarvis became a student of Chagdud Tulku Rinpoche, word began spreading throughout the world's Buddhist communities about a death row prisoner who was studying under the great lama. It spread further when he became Pema's student, and his reputation grew more when she wrote about him in her books and mentioned him in her lectures. In the years that followed, more Buddhist students, practitioners, nuns, and monks wrote, and many visited him. A guard once told Pamela that Jarvis's list of approved visitors was the longest on death row.

Jarvis enjoyed most of the visitors, and he learned from many. However, some of them confused and overwhelmed him. He once complained to Hozan Alan Senauke, a Sōtō Zen priest and vice-abbot of the Berkeley Zen Center who'd become a close friend, "Some of these cats show up all swami-ed out, pushing their spiritual trips on me. They come on like they're Buddha himself. But it's like they're tourists—death row is some exotic destination. They collect trophies and are looking for a con on death row for their display case."

Many of the supposedly highly evolved Buddhists were patronizing, telling him that he was doing Buddhism all wrong: "I'm not meditating right, reading the right books, not getting what it's about." He was disappointed because he'd expected advanced practitioners to inspire him with their humility, wisdom, and grace.

In response, Alan offered a Zen koan for him to ponder, explaining it was from Chinese Zen master Lin Chi, who'd said, "If you meet a buddha, kill the buddha." Alan explained: "So think about that: kill the Buddha."

"Kill the Buddha?" Jarvis asked. *"Why? How?"* When Alan saw his puzzlement, he smiled at Jarvis, and then he said, "Let the answer come to you. Just relax."

Buddhist monks and practitioners continued to flock to death row to meet Jarvis. Joe Baxter sent Baba Ram Dass, the former Harvard professor and Timothy Leary sidekick who'd authored the seminal 1970s spiritual guidebook *Be Here Now.* Jarvis was impressed by Ram Dass—if only because he somehow convinced the guards to let him walk barefoot into San Quentin.

Another time, Joe sent a monk, an American kid with his shaved head, beads, sandals, and red robes—the whole getup. When the monk spoke, Jarvis realized that he was just another pompous fraud trying to bestow wisdom like the guru he was not.

The monk droned on, boasting about his travels to Tibet and India and his meeting with the Dalai Lama. Jarvis felt what he'd felt when other allegedly evolved Buddhists had visited: that their kind of arrogance was antithetical to Buddhism. The monk was making him mad, and he was tempted to end the visit early.

After a while, the monk looked across the room at the wall of vending machines and announced that he wanted a Coke. Jarvis summoned the guard, who let him out of the cage. Jarvis watched him approach a machine and put quarters into the slot. Nothing happened. The monk shook the machine. Again, nothing. Then he reared back and kicked the machine with shocking ferocity.

Everyone in the hall stared at the monk. A guard glanced at Jarvis and shook his head.

The monk returned, held out his empty hands, and sighed. "The machine stole my money," he said before resuming his homily about peace, tranquility, and detachment.

Jarvis interrupted him. "Wait a minute," he said. "You're talking about enlightenment and detachment and all that, so what were you doing trying to kill that machine? What was that about?"

The monk looked at him as if the answer were obvious. "I wanted my Coke."

Jarvis laughed and realized that, amid all the lecturing, the monk was teaching him a lesson he hadn't planned to teach. The man's robes, his preaching, were his protection against his own confusion. He wasn't some high, egoless being who'd transcended desire and was unbothered by the trivialities of life. He knew more Tibetan words than Jarvis did, but otherwise the two of them weren't that different. The monk was clinging desperately to his Buddhist practice because he needed it to keep him afloat in the world. Jarvis looked at the monk again and saw someone who struggled and suffered, as we all do. Empathy welled up inside Jarvis, and he enjoyed the rest of the visit.

When it ended and Jarvis was being escorted back to the tier, he looked over his shoulder at the departing monk in his flowing robes. Jarvis understood why he'd become so annoyed and angry at that guy and the other condescending monks who visited him—because of how badly he wanted them to be what some envisioned themselves to be: an incarnation of Buddha come to save him.

The meaning of the koan Alan had offered dawned on him. He didn't know if it was the correct meaning, but each of his teachers had given him permission to interpret Buddhism in whatever way worked for him. He'd seen how Buddhism meets you wherever you are and lets you take what you can from it at that moment. In fact, it was unlike other faiths in that there weren't rules, and even its most fundamental precepts were infinitely flexible. But in spite of all that, he still envisioned the Buddha as a kind of deity sitting on a mountaintop, having transcended suffering. He wanted Buddha to lift him up out of San Quentin onto that mountaintop, high above his suffering—to save him. That's the Buddha he had to kill—the illusion that anything outside ourselves can save us. What he learned is that Buddha can't save us. Jesus can't. Allah can't. Only we can save ourselves.

PART THREE

THE THIRD NOBLE TRUTH

THE END OF SUFFERING

We have spent a lifetime developing responses to pain and difficulty. Changing these old habits is like trying to reverse the momentum of a boulder tumbling down a mountainside. It requires great effort, skill, patience, perseverance, and no small amount of courage.

—Lama Shenpen (Lisa Leghorn)

10

CONNECTION

In addition to moving forward on the appeal, Baxter and the other lawyers had been working to get Jarvis moved out of the Adjustment Center. Studies have shown that solitary confinement is psychologically damaging, though it doesn't take research to see the damage that weeks, let alone months, years, and decades, spent alone in a box can inflict. Courts have ruled that solitary confinement is cruel and unusual punishment. A UN report concluded that a stay longer than fifteen days in isolation "amounts to torture." Jarvis had been in the hole for twenty-two years.

The Jarvistas had also mounted a campaign to get the prison to release him from the AC. His supporters wrote to the San Quentin warden, representatives of the California Department of Corrections and Rehabilitation, and politicians. One afternoon Scott Kauffman brought Marie copies of letters that had been sent to the warden; there were hundreds from all around the world. Marie and Pamela met with the San Quentin ombudsman, county officials, and state legislators. However, citing his criminal history and past gang affiliation, the prison ignored all the letters and inquiries and for years denied the lawyers' requests.

Finally, in March 2007, Jarvis was roused one morning and told to get ready. The lawyers' and his supporters' efforts had finally paid off; he was getting out of solitary at last.

"One coming down!"

The words echoed through the cavernous cellblock. Waiting for the "all clear" from ground-floor security, a guard held on to Jarvis's upper arm and led him out of the AC, escorting him to East Block, where he locked him in a smaller cell. The first thing Jarvis noticed in East Block was the deafening noise. The AC had its own din, but mostly it was muted by solid cell doors. Here, where cell doors were bars and mesh, sound traveled and mingled—a cacophony of yelling, alarms, buzzers, calls to guards over loudspeakers, banging cell doors, and blaring TVs and radios. Jarvis had had seizures when he was a child—the first when he learned that Mamie Procks had died. He hadn't had one in a decade, but that first night in East Block, he had the worst seizure of his life.

All he'd wanted for two decades was to get out of the AC, but now, feeling exposed and overwhelmed, all he wanted to do was return.

* * *

Over his twenty-two years in the AC, Jarvis had been allowed time outside only in a small yard or a walk-alone cage, similar to a dog kennel. In those confines he'd been able to take a dozen or so paces, and he walked that distance countless thousands of times. The first time out in the East Block yard, Jarvis took ten steps and froze. Finally he took a deep breath and a step forward, then another.

Whenever he panicked on East Block, Jarvis meditated, and he slowly acclimated to his new home. He came to relish using a real toothbrush instead of the nub of one (a toothbrush handle could be honed into a weapon); a tube of toothpaste rather than a tiny dab in a paper cup. Melody brought him a string of real lacquered-wood mala beads. With some nostalgia, he set aside his string of aspirin.

In a cell with a bunk bolted to the wall (as opposed to the concrete slab he'd had in the AC), he had what felt like infinitely more space, because he could store his possessions under the bed. He was allowed gifts prohibited in the AC. Ordering from a prison-approved concessionaire, Pamela and Marty sent him a new TV and a CD player. They also sent him an electric teakettle, which he used to boil water for Top Ramen and instant coffee from the commissary.

For more than twenty years, all of Jarvis's letters and stories and his book had been handwritten with the inserts of pens. In East Block, he was allowed another present from Pamela: an IBM Selectric typewriter.

Jarvis decorated his cell with photos of his mother and friends, postcards they'd sent from their travels around the world, posters of Bob Marley, Jimi Hendrix, and Pam Greer, and an image of the Buddha.

He had money on his account funded by the Krasneys and other friends, and he used it to buy candy, chips, the ramen, and other snacks. He started a jailhouse charity, trading Mars, Snickers, and Kit Kat bars for postage stamps. Whenever he amassed fifty dollars' worth of stamps, he sent them to Human Kindness Foundation, a nonprofit that traded stamps for books for prisoners.

The AC yard had a basketball court, but it was pathetic—a cracked and weedy dirt surface, bent rims, no nets. In contrast, the East Block yard had a full-size court with new nets and freshly chalked white lines. For Jarvis, it was the Staples Center.

Of the new privileges, the ones that mattered most to Jarvis were new ways to connect with his friends. He could request the use of a phone, which would be delivered to his cell on a cart. He called friends who set up prepaid accounts with the prison's telephone contractor, and they talked in fifteen-minute intervals (the maximum time per call), sometimes for hours.

The most extraordinary new privilege had to do with visits. In the AC, where scratched and dirty glass had separated him from his visitors, the closest he could get to physical contact was two hands placed on opposite sides of the window. In East Block he had contact visits. He'd be escorted to a small cage with bars covered with Plexiglas in a grouping of similar cages that recalled an old-fashioned circus—as if the enclosures had been occupied by black bears and Siberian tigers instead of men. There were a table and plastic chairs inside the cage. Guards would lock him in and unchain him. His hands freed, he and his friends could touch, even hug.

The first time Pema came to see him in his new home, she and Jarvis just looked at each other for a moment. They broke into wide grins and embraced.

And then Marie came. They were allowed to hug when they met and again when they parted. For the rest of the visit, they were limited to holding hands, but they cherished feeling each other's warmth and pulse. One day Marie said aloud what they'd both been thinking: she was falling in love with him.

Jarvis was overwhelmed to realize that she shared his feelings. He said he felt it, too.

Their confessions didn't change their letters and meetings materially, but they felt different. They both felt shier, vulnerable. Jarvis was joyful, though he wasn't sure if he could trust the good feelings to last.

Jarvis had fantasized about asking Marie to marry him for half a year before he was released from the AC, but he'd been too nervous to propose. What would a marriage mean between two people separated from each other by a thick sheet of glass? Her expression of love was one thing, but he worried that she'd reject him. He didn't want to chase her away by coming on too strong. However, when he was free from the AC, no longer kept apart from Marie by the wall between them, he mustered the nerve and got on one knee and asked. She didn't say anything at first.

She smiled and teared up. "I will," she said. "But I think we should get married in the free air. When you're out."

Jarvis's heart was pounding.

*   *   *

It had never dawned on Marie that Jarvis *wouldn't* get out. He was innocent, and justice would prevail. It *had* to. After working tirelessly to free him from solitary, she joined Pamela and others who were fighting for his exoneration. She often imagined him walking out of San Quentin. That's when they should get married. But she changed her mind when Rick Targow told her that even if Jarvis prevailed in the coming hearing, it could be years before he'd be released. She also learned that as his wife, she could call the prison and check up on him if there was a lockdown or he was ill. As a legal spouse, she could make inquiries about his legal case and make medical decisions if he couldn't do so himself.

So she agreed not to wait.

They had two June weddings. First they were married by a prison chaplain in a ceremony recognized by the state. A week later Pema came to perform a traditional Tibetan Buddhist marriage ceremony, though modified for death row. Normally the ceremony is conducted with six bowls, each holding an offering that symbolizes the virtues of a good marriage. The bowls weren't allowed into the prison, so in preparation Marie placed bowls that contained the offerings—a flower, incense, a candle, perfumed water, food, and a small bell—on her kitchen table at home. She photographed each bowl and ordered prints.

On the day of the wedding, Marie placed the six photographs in a circle on the wooden table in the cage. The table became an altar. She and Jarvis held hands as Pema asked the couple to commit to cultivating "generosity, kindness, enthusiasm, discipline, wisdom, patience, and most of all, compassion, not only for yourselves but for all beings." She said, "The most important thing is for you to be kind to each other."

When the ceremony was over, the on-duty guard took a photo of the newlyweds. Then they and Pema shared Hostess cupcakes from the vending machine.

Jarvis admitted that he'd never had a committed relationship that lasted long and didn't know if he knew how to. At twelve, he was introduced to sex by a girl who'd been introduced to sex by an uncle. As a boy in Harbor City and in juvenile lockups, Jarvis had had girlfriends, but those relationships didn't last. He reflected back on whether he'd ever seen a man treat women kindly and lovingly. There was one: Dennis Procks, who'd doted on Mamie. That was all he could think of. Otherwise he'd been told to respect women by men who beat their girlfriends, wives, and daughters. He'd seen girls being slapped, thrown out of their homes, and called whores by their mothers, who *were* whores, and their fathers, who were pimps. His mother had been abused by one violent man after another.

Years earlier, he and Melody had talked a lot about masculinity, and she'd given him books on the subject. In one of those discussions, she'd asked him, "What does a boy learn about women from a mother who was a prostitute, who sometimes offered love but sometimes withheld it, who was violent and failed to protect her son from violent men?"

Jarvis looked grave. "You don't have a lot of trust," he said, "and you don't necessarily become somebody who can be trusted. You learn to run. You leave before you're left."

Now that he was married, Jarvis talked about his fears with Pema. "I'm afraid I'll blow it," he confided.

They talked for a while before Pema said, "I was thinking about something you told me once, how badly you felt because you didn't protect your mother from your father and other men. You also felt you should have protected your sisters. You felt that guilt even though you couldn't have protected them; you were just a child. Regardless of whether it's logical or not, maybe you feel you don't deserve a woman's trust."

Jarvis said, "This with Marie is different than anything I've ever felt. I want it to be different."

Pema said, "*You* are different. You aren't the same person you were."

As the months went by, the question hung in the air, and meanwhile Jarvis and Marie were challenged in ways other couples aren't. There are no honeymoons on death row. They saw each other as often as possible, talked on the phone when they could, and wrote countless letters, but they had no privacy; their visits were monitored, and their letters were read. Sometimes they couldn't speak or see each other for weeks or months because of lockdowns. Marie worried about him when there was violence in the prison, and she couldn't help him when he was ill. But it was all right, she told herself. It *would be* all right. It would be all right when he got out.

11

FORGIVENESS

"Mama, I wrote my father."

Pema was at her abbey in Nova Scotia, where she spent half the year, when she received Jarvis's letter.

"Writing him was one of Marie's arm-twisting moves," he continued. "He wrote back, told me about his problems—diabetes, kidney stones, heart attack. I was pissed off at him, but he wants to visit me. I'm not sure if I want to see him."

Jarvis had heard from his father, Harline Masters, only once in more than twenty years. He'd visited Jarvis soon after he'd been imprisoned, but not since. Jarvis told Marie to tell him no, the man was an SOB, but she pointed out that his father was old and ailing and it might be his last chance to see the man. He agreed to let him visit.

*　　*　　*

Back in the late 1980s, when Melody was writing the social history of Jarvis's life, she'd asked about his father, and he recounted stories about his violence. He'd told Melody about the night he hid under the bed when Harline beat Cynthia and threatened to kill him and his sisters. Other times Harline had threatened him and his siblings with a straight-edged razor, and once, in a fit of anger, he set the house on fire. Jarvis's aunt and uncle arrived to find the children screaming inside the burning home.

Harline left them soon after, and he'd had almost no contact with his son since then. During the penalty phase of the murder trial, when Melody tracked Harline down to interview him, he'd asked her for money.

At the time she was working on the report and Jarvis told her about his father's violence, Melody had said, "He was a terrible father."

Jarvis's reaction shocked her. "Maybe he wasn't a terrible father," he said. "Maybe he was the *best* father."

"What are you talking about?" Melody asked. "He *hurt* you. He *abandoned* you."

"But what are fathers supposed to do?" Jarvis continued. "A good father doesn't give you what you want, he gives you what you need. Fathers are supposed to protect their children, and that's what he did."

"But he *terrorized* you!"

"When he did, he gave me a gift. He gave me hate. I *needed* that hate. Hate for my father helped me survive. I wouldn't be alive if it weren't for that hate."

He could see she was still mystified, so he explained: "Every time I fought someone on the street, when I was attacked and I fought back, giving more than I got; when violent counselors and foster parents and whoever else it was tried to break me down, and I took their abuse and smiled a smile that made them hit me harder or throw me onto the floor and kick me, my father gave me rage, and rage is the reason I'm alive."

He pressed his eyes closed. "If I'd have let myself feel fear, I'd be dead. He taught me what it means to be a real man: Fearless. Hard. Fighting."

Melody nodded her head. Then she quietly asked, "But is a real man someone who hates like that, fights like that, or is a real man kind, loving, a good provider to his children?"

Jarvis replied, "Now, that is a question no one ever asked me."

Harline was born in Waco, Texas, while his father—Jarvis's grandfather—was in jail in California for stealing cattle and forgery. Harline followed his parents to California and, when he was old enough, enlisted in the army. After being discharged, he moved to Southern California. One night, he drove to a party in a car with the words LOVE BANDIT painted on the back fender. That night he met Cynthia Campbell.

A few weeks after they met, they got married in spite of Cynthia's mother's warning to Harline that her daughter was trouble.

Cynthia already had Tommy and Robbie. Harline and Cynthia had Charlene and then Jarvis, who was born in 1962, and then Birdy. Harline left them in 1967.

When Jarvis agreed to see Harline, Marie made the arrangements. On the morning of the visit, Jarvis was nervous. When he arrived at the visiting cage, he saw that Marie was alone. She told him that Harline had canceled. He had a bowling tournament, and he could win a lot of money.

Jarvis was furious. "A bowling tournament?" he asked incredulously. He felt like a fool for agreeing to see his father, but then Harline's words replayed in his head, and he couldn't help but laugh. He felt strangely elated. "How can I be mad at a father who hadn't seen his son in all those years and then cancels because of a bowling tournament?" He thought of a Buddhist saying: "You can't expect a stone not to be a stone." He laughed again.

A week after he canceled, Harline called Marie and asked if she'd schedule another visit. Marie relayed the message to Jarvis, who said no.

"Can't you forgive him?" she asked. "He's old. He's sick."

Jarvis said, "There's too much damage. Those memories . . . I've been thinking about it. What he did to my mother. My sisters. Me. I have no reason to see him."

But over the next six months, Marie convinced him. She repeated her point that this visit might be Jarvis's last chance to see his father.

*   *   *

On the appointed morning, Jarvis waited in the cage. He wouldn't have been surprised if Harline didn't show up again, but eventually he did, dressed in his work uniform. Along with running a one-man recycling business—Harline collected cans and bottles in the back of an old pickup truck—he worked as a crossing guard at a grammar school, and everything he wore was yellow: a washed-out yellow polo shirt, yellow pants with fluorescent yellow stripes down the legs, and a yellow windbreaker.

When he saw his son, Harline belted out, "Jay!" That's what he'd called Jarvis when he was a boy. Their eyes met, and for Jarvis it was like looking in a mirror.

A guard let Harline and Marie into the cage and locked the door. Jarvis hugged Marie, then looked at his father again and said, "Hey." They exchanged a perfunctory hug.

Harline nodded in a sort of bow. "Son," he said.

They sat down, and Harline stated the obvious: "It's been a hell of a long time."

Jarvis smiled. "Yeah."

Jarvis labored to reconcile the old man before him with the monster who'd beaten him, collapsed in crack-induced stupors, and ultimately abandoned his family.

For some reason, perhaps the Buddhist practice that had taught him to face his hardest recollections head-on, Jarvis brought up that that beating now. "I'll tell you what I think about when I think of you," he said. "That night . . ." He recounted the time Cynthia hid Jarvis and his siblings while Harline rampaged, beating her and threatening to kill the kids. "I was under the bed the whole time," he said. "Watching. Listening."

Harline looked confused. He removed his glasses, pressed his fingers to his eyes, and replaced the glasses. After a moment, he spoke. "I never did that. That wasn't me." He stared at Jarvis. "Those were somebody else's shoes. It wasn't me."

Jarvis was flustered. At first he thought Harline was lying. But then he had a jarring vision, almost as if a slideshow of images played inside his head. He saw his mother look out the window. He heard her. "It's Daddy!" she yelled. "Pack your things!"

Jarvis recalled all the "daddys." Cynthia called some men who visited—some for a night, some for longer—"daddy" or "uncle." "Say hello to Daddy," she'd tell her kids, or "This is Uncle Bobby."

He mused, *I was only four years old. What does a four-year-old really know? What if that man wasn't my father?*

So much in his life was built on the memory of those shoes. Rage at his father, hatred of his father lay behind every blow he'd landed on anyone: kids on the street and in lockups, men in prison.

Jarvis reminded himself of all the pain that was certainly his father's doing—the beatings, the neglect—but none of it really mattered to him at that moment. Now his father was an old man in a bowling league who worked as a crossing guard. He'd spent years addicted to crack, but as they talked, Jarvis learned that he was clean now. He'd had a girlfriend for thirty years, but she'd died. He was raising his step-granddaughter.

And here he was now, with his son. Jarvis's rage and hate? He knew they weren't gone. Eliminating them completely would take more time and work. But he felt something pure and unexpected, a kind of heat in the room. In his father's face, Jarvis saw a faint glow.

Then a guard came over and announced that time was up. Jarvis stood and began to thank his father for coming, but Harline was already in the guard's face. "I need more time with my son. I haven't seen him in years."

The guard was respectful but firm. "I'm sorry, sir. Visiting time's over."

"The hell it is!" Harline said. "I'm not going."

Jarvis looked at his father and smiled. "It's okay," he said. "It's the rules."

Jarvis said, "Come here." This time he hugged Harline tightly. Was his father crying? Jarvis held him for a few moments more and let go. But Harline clung to his son, and tears came to Jarvis, too.

After Harline left, Jarvis thought about his yelling at the guard and realized it was the first time his father had ever fought for him. That brought on a new moment of lightness. Later that day, back in his cell, Jarvis folded his blanket, laid it on the floor, and sat down to meditate. He was filled with the joy of . . . of forgiveness. He felt something he'd never imagined he could feel for his father: an eddy of something he could barely identify but eventually did. The feeling was love for that old man.

Pema was delighted when Jarvis told her about Harline's visit, and she recounted a classic Buddhist tale about a monk traveling with a student. They were preparing to cross a river when a woman approached and said the current was too strong for her to make it on her own. The older monk picked the woman up, carried her across the river on his shoulders, placed her gently on the other side, and resumed his journey.

His student was perplexed, because monks of that order weren't allowed to touch women. He caught up with his teacher and asked, "How could you carry that woman on your shoulders?"

The monk replied, "I set her down when we got to the other side of the river. You're still carrying her."

Pema asked, "How long have you carried your father?"

It was a palpable relief to feel he didn't have to anymore.

The experience led to a series of conversations with Pema about forgiveness, and she suggested that he make a list of the people he'd hated most throughout his life. It was long. In many cases, his hatred was justified. Who wouldn't hate those who'd beaten him, separated him from his family, made him fight, and burned, abandoned, and betrayed him? Who wouldn't hate supposed friends who had betrayed him and accused him of committing a terrible crime he hadn't committed, those who prosecuted him for that crime, a jury that found him guilty of committing that crime, and a judge who sentenced him to death? There were many others: violent relatives and foster parents, psychologists and social workers who promised to help him but hadn't, counselors and jailers, and on and on.

As Pema instructed, while he meditated Jarvis focused on each of the people, one at a time. He started with the ones who'd hurt him in his youth. Rage engulfed him when he pictured them and their cruelty. Each time it was like falling into a nightmare. But as Pema promised, at some point he recognized that he was in a story, sitting in meditation, and he did what she taught him to do with the pause: he breathed. Freed from the story, he returned to his body. He sat with the person again and looked into their eyes. In every case, he saw what he'd never seen before. Below the wrath and violence, he saw suffering. When he saw the pain, his swirling fury began to evaporate.

Anger washed over him anew when he got to the prosecutors, the jurors, and the witnesses who had lied about him, convicting him and sentencing him to death. He knew the loathing was justified in those cases. However, when he made himself look into their eyes, too, he saw them differently. He saw sadness, loneliness, and confusion. He saw their scars. His hatred morphed into something like tenderness, though sometimes the good feeling didn't last. When he imagined their faces again, his anger flared. He thought, *Their suffering doesn't excuse the pain they inflicted on me. They destroyed my life.* He thought of something Pema once said: we change in fits and starts; there's no rushing it. He thought, *I can't forgive them. Not yet.*

It was even more complicated when he got to Judge Savitt. Of those who put him on death row, he thought most often about her. During the trial he'd sometimes seen her as a kind of mother figure, but he also recalled her hard, masklike face before she issued the death sentence. While meditating, though, he saw a scared girl beneath the mask.

At the sentencing hearing, Jarvis remembered her saying that she didn't believe in the death penalty but her job required her to ignore her conscience and follow the law. He saw she was conflicted and confused and imagined her after his trial. If she didn't believe in the death penalty, he wondered, had it been hard to live with the knowledge that she'd condemned a man to death?

When Judge Savitt sentenced him, she acknowledged that deciding the punishment was the most difficult decision she'd ever faced. She felt compelled to affirm the sentence, but he understood that she had struggled against her obligation. "When people try and fail, it's easier to forgive them than when they don't try," he told Pema when they next spoke. "In Judge Savitt's face I saw her confusion, even her fear. It's hard to stay angry after that. It's not that I don't still blame her sometimes. I don't know if I can completely forgive her, either. But when I think of her and see her as a person like the rest of us, flawed, trying to get through life, it feels different."

"That feeling," Pema said, "is compassion."

12

ANOTHER WAY

Jarvis called Pema later that week to catch her up on the latest events on death row. A week earlier he was on the yard and saw his best and oldest friend, Freddie Taylor. After having been convicted of first-degree murder and sentenced to death in 1985, Freddie was in the AC when Jarvis, charged with the Burchfield murder, was moved there. The two men had similar histories. Like Jarvis, Freddie had grown up in state institutions, including reform schools where he'd been subjected to violence like what Jarvis experienced. Almost all the kids in Freddie's reform school were white. He thought his name was "Nigger" until he was seven or eight years old. Before being transferred to San Quentin, Freddie was in Folsom Prison, where, like Jarvis, he was trained by and accepted into the BGF. He was given the name Yero, Swahili for "born a soldier."

Jarvis was at his hardest and meanest then, pissed off about the murder charge, pissed off in general, fighting inmates and guards, training as a BGF soldier. He'd embraced the political education and indoctrination, and he relished his position in one of the most powerful gangs in San Quentin.

The BGF and their backgrounds weren't all they had in common. They shared a sense of humor. When they got going, they laughed so much and so loud that people on the yard told them to shut the fuck up, which made them laugh more.

Freddie saw Jarvis soon after Cynthia died, and consoled his friend, and he encouraged Jarvis when his murder trial commenced— and again when he was condemned. Throughout that period Jarvis supported Freddie, too, when a date was set for his execution and when it was scheduled again after Freddie's lawyers got a postponement. Jarvis helped Freddie stay positive. "It's going to be okay. Just hold on."

When Freddie learned that Jarvis was meditating, he was dubious. "What kind of con game is this?" He became downright insulting when Jarvis began talking about Buddhism. "You're fucking kidding me, right?" Freddie said. "A fucking Buddhist? You gonna pray to that fat motherfucker? This is horseshit."

But Freddie noticed Jarvis changing. At first he couldn't put his finger on what was different, but eventually he realized that his friend wasn't seething all the time, wasn't angry, wasn't looking to fight. Freddie thought about the way most men responded to their death sentences. Many started out angry, and over time their rage took them over completely. Jarvis still had his moments when his anger flared—one day he cursed out a guard again and spent several weeks in a quiet cell. But those events were rare, and as most men on the row spiraled down down down—getting meaner, crazier—Jarvis was becoming a fucking Buddhist! Freddie was cynical about the changes for a long time, but his cynicism changed to bafflement when he saw Jarvis do things on the yard that prisoners never did—things that could get him killed.

Jarvis came out on the yard one foggy morning and saw Freddie in intense conversation with a group of other cons. He approached his old friend from behind and said, "What's up, ugly?" Freddie turned and yelled, "Left!" and they embraced.

Despite Freddie's delight in seeing Jarvis, Jarvis could tell he was distracted. Freddie moved away from the group and stood close to Jarvis as he looked across the yard and pointed out a man huddled by the fence. "Fag is going to be hit," Freddie said. "They're doing him—a rat. Told the guards about [he named the con] for hassling him. He's a dead man."

Freddie saw Jarvis's face change to horror. "They can't kill him," Jarvis said.

The response startled Freddie. "Why the fuck not?"

Jarvis was quiet for a minute and then said, "It's what the cops want them to do. It's how they've always done us. Get us fighting among ourselves. We can't fall into that trap."

Freddie watched as Jarvis moved across the yard toward the con. By talking to him Jarvis was risking his own life, and Freddie prepared to jump in to protect his friend. But no one moved on him. Jarvis came back and said the guy *hadn't* snitched, he'd been set up.

Freddie responded, "What the fuck do you think he's going to say? He's going to tell you he's a snitch? No one wants to hear that. Motherfucker is not long for this world."

Without a word, Jarvis left Freddie and went over to the three men poised to attack the con. He greeted the two older men, whom he knew, and then said, "Listen: Cops are setting the fish up. They want us to take him out."

The men were stunned. But Jarvis went on, "They're trying to use us as their enforcers. Don't fall for it. They hate him because he's gay. It's sport for them. Get us fighting, killing."

"What the fuck?" the young con said. "Who the fuck are you, old man?"

Jarvis said, "I've been here a fuck of a long time. You weren't born when I got here." He looked directly into the boy's eyes. "Listen. Cops are counting on you to be who you've always been. You react. No questions. No thought. Bullets fly. You're in the hole. Someone's dead. Stop and think."

"I think," the boy said, "I think you are a pussy."

There was a time when that word would have triggered Jarvis, and he would have proved he was no pussy on the spot. The kid would have been on the ground. Jarvis thought of all the trouble he'd gotten into by proving he wasn't a pussy. Here was a boy trying to be a badass like he was taking on some OG. Jarvis smiled at the boy.

By then Freddie had joined the group, and Jarvis turned to him and the other men. "You know it's true," Jarvis said. "Cops want that boy dead, and they can't do it. You really want to work for those fuckers?"

The boy said, "He's a fucking *faggot*."

Jarvis said, "See, the way it works in here, the wolves are going to prey on the sheep. That punk's a sheep. We have to protect the sheep."

Freddie was mystified when he saw the men's reactions. They'd gone from hard and determined to . . . calm. One of the old-timers looked at the young con and, referring to Jarvis, said, "You gotta watch out for this motherfucker. He'll fuck with your mind. The motherfucking Buddhist of death row."

The older men laughed.

One asked, "Hey, Left, you see the game?" The San Francisco Giants were in the playoffs. The men began talking about baseball, and for the moment the gay kid was safe.

"What the fuck is all this?" Freddie asked when he and Jarvis were alone again. "You're like some motherfucker with a force field around you?" First he'd thought Jarvis had been dangerously reckless when he put himself in the middle of a likely stabbing, but he realized it was the opposite. The image of a force field wasn't completely off the mark. Jarvis now radiated a kind of power—not the power normally respected in the prison, which was based on fear and control, but something else. Jarvis had the power to make people stop. Stop and think.

Freddie said, "So this is what a Buddhist is, huh? Peace and shit. Nonviolence."

Jarvis shrugged. "I just know that killing leads to more killing. It's what we always lived." He referred to the neighborhoods in which they'd grown up. "All revenge," he said. "You know how it went down. *Still* goes down. 'You dissed me, I'll take you out.' 'You shot at my sister, I'll kill your mother.' We all been there. 'My father is beating my mother, I'm going to kill the SOB.' But thinking on that track is dangerous, because what else does it justify? 'Not only will I kill my father, I will kill whoever stops me from killing my father.'" Jarvis asked, "Where does that end?"

"So that's your fucking Buddhist trip," Freddie said. He closed his eyes, held his palms together as if in prayer, and teased, "Ommm."

Jarvis laughed and said, "Buddhism teaches you there's always another way."

When he was alone in his cell that night, Jarvis thought back on the afternoon and, confused and a little afraid, asked himself, *What were you thinking?* He'd never done anything that risky before. Freddie had said he could have been stabbed for putting himself in the middle, and Jarvis knew he was right. But when he was intervening, he'd never considered the threat. His actions had been automatic, as if he'd been compelled.

Growing up, both Freddie and Jarvis smoked pot and sniffed glue and paint, but Freddie's drug use escalated, and he'd become addicted to heroin, methamphetamine, and other drugs. Over the years in San Quentin, Freddie had multiple overdoses that almost killed him, but he was a survivor. The ODs shook him up, and each time he got clean and stayed sober for a while. Freddie had been clean for maybe half a year when Jarvis saw him on the yard again and knew he'd relapsed bad. Freddie's eyes were glassy, his pupils were pinholes, and his body vibrated.

Jarvis went over and gave Freddie a hug. "What's going down, brother?" he asked.

Freddie pushed him away, but Jarvis whispered into his ear, "It's all right, man. We're going to get on this."

"On what?" Freddie snapped. "What the fuck are you talking about?"

Jarvis repeated, "We're going to do it. We're getting clean."

Freddie pulled back and glowered. "What's this 'we' bullshit?"

Jarvis said, "Yero, if you fail, we fail. We are in this together."

Freddie thought Jarvis was full of shit when he started talking that way, and he became angry when Jarvis suggested meditation. Jarvis said, "Just try. You have nothing to lose." Freddie said, "No fucking way." He went back to his cell and got high.

The next day Freddie came out again, and Jarvis approached him. Freddie could barely talk. Slurring, he said, "I've done time for most of my life. I've had two execution dates. My family is mostly dead. My sister is sixteen hundred miles away. I got no visitors; no one writes me. The craving is strong. I'm a junkie. That's who I am."

A couple of weeks later, Freddie began receiving letters: one, two, then a dozen—people asking about him, checking up on him, offering to help. Freddie didn't understand why it was happening until one of the writers said she knew Jarvis, and he realized that Jarvis had asked them to contact him. Freddie replied to their letters and began corresponding regularly with some of them.

Jarvis asked Freddie to try meditation again. "Just try, brother. For me." He said, "Listen. I hated all this Buddhist shit—all the talk about suffering, death, facing your shit. The thing is, the shit chases you until you face it. Meditation helps you face it. That's all it's about. In here it will help more than anything else you could do."

He instructed him: "So you sit and breathe. Breathe in through your nose. Deep. Fill your lungs. Feel it. Hold it a second and slowly let it out. Your mind will wander. When it does, just focus on your breath again."

When they were on the yard together again a few days later, Freddie said he was doing it, at least trying. "This meditation bullshit feels good," he said.

A few days after that, Jarvis asked Freddie if he'd thought about getting clean again. Freddie responded, "I think about it all the time."

"Shall we try?"

Freddie rolled his eyes—"we" again—and that night he had a packet of heroin sent down the tier by fishline.

A week after that, a booklet was delivered to Freddie's cell. Jarvis had asked Pamela to send him a Buddhist adaptation of the traditional twelve steps, which Freddie brought out to the yard the next day. He asked Jarvis, "What the fuck is this?"

"Let's do this thing," Jarvis said. "See what it's all about."

The two men sat together and read. Those Buddhist twelve steps replaced the basic precepts of Alcoholics Anonymous, such as one's powerlessness over their addiction and the requirement that a person turn their life over to a higher power, with a series of meditations and contemplations. Jarvis read them aloud, and he and Freddie discussed them. The first, called *samma-sankappa*, was meditating "with the intention that is motivated by love, compassion, and a desire to transform our lives." There'd been a time Jarvis couldn't imagine sitting on the yard. He'd told Melody that sitting was dangerous in prison. But now he didn't think twice about sitting—he didn't care that cons and guards stared and made jokes—and Freddie followed his lead. They sat on a bench, not the ground, and Jarvis guided his friend. "Breathe," he said. "Think about those words. Love, compassion. Think about the fact that you want to change your life and realize that you can."

Then Jarvis suggested that Freddie try to meditate whenever he felt the urge to get high. "It'll be hard," Jarvis said. "It'll be fucking hard. The feeling will start, but there'll be a pause." He felt he was channeling Pema. "That pause gives you a chance to look at what's happening. When you do, you interrupt it. Recognize the feeling. Allow yourself to feel it as you watch it. Then try breathing through the craving. See if you can breathe it away. Feel it go away."

Freddie practiced that week and reported his progress to Jarvis. "I broke down," he said one day. "Copped and got high. It's just too fucking hard. The jonesing. Can't do." Freddie's face had a red-purple bruise that ran from his forehead to his ear.

"What the fuck?" Jarvis asked. "What happened?"

Freddie said last night he was sure it was his time to be executed, and he tried to kill himself by smashing his head against the wall.

"So sorry, man," Jarvis said. "That's hard. I'm so sorry. We're not done. That drug makes you crazy, paranoid. It happens. It's just a bump, man. We are going to take this on. No judgment. It happens. It's a bear. We did it before and we'll do it again. You're doing great, man, you're doing great."

Jarvis read the next of the Buddhist 12 Steps, *samma-sati*, which involved mindfulness meditation "to develop complete awareness of oneself, feelings, thoughts, people, surroundings, and reality." Jarvis explained, "The craving will come. Like before, when you recognize it, breathe in. Focus on what's going on inside and out: thoughts, anxiety, noise, smells, and coldness. The craving hits again. Breathe in again. Return to what's inside and outside. Just do the best you can."

A week later, Freddie told him he was going to do it, get clean. Really. This time for sure. There was no gentle, medication-assisted detoxing in prison. It had to be done cold turkey, which meant there was no avoiding the hell, but he'd gone through it before. Freddie braced himself that night. As Jarvis suggested, he sat in meditation. The craving came, and he toppled over. Feverish and shivering, he curled up on the floor. He thought of Jarvis and pushed himself upright, sat erect, and breathed. He began convulsing. He cried. When the paroxysms subsided, he meditated again—just a few minutes, but it calmed him. He went like that for thirty hours. After that he stayed in his cell two more days before returning to the yard. When he saw Jarvis, he gave his friend a bear hug. "We've done it," he said with a huge smile.

On the six-month anniversary of Freddie's sobriety, Jarvis presented him with candy bars Pamela had sent in a care package. "Proud of you, my brother." The two men ate Snickers in the sun.

By then Jarvis had learned that on the Buddhist path there's progress and regression, and regression can be progress and vice versa. As Pema told him, "It's not like we learn something in Buddhism, pass a test, and move on to the next state of being." We can regress because of the internal process of changing and awakening; we may grasp a profound idea and then lose it. And sometimes it happens that life throws a wrench into our practice.

Several months after the celebration with Freddie, a pair of guards came to Jarvis's cell and told him he was being moved. "What the hell?" Jarvis said.

The new cell reeked. Jarvis looked around and saw why: the walls were smeared with shit, and there were pools of piss on the floor. He looked at the guard. "No fucking way. You've got to be fucking kidding."

When Jarvis first arrived in San Quentin, he was put in a grimy cell. There were cockroaches, the walls and floors were dirty, and it smelled of urine. Jarvis stuffed toilet paper into the cracks in the walls to keep out the roaches, and he spent the night and following day cleaning until the cell was spotless. As bad as that was, this was far worse.

In the past Jarvis would have cursed out the guard, at least. If he could have gotten his hands on him, he would have assaulted him. But he stopped himself from reacting. Instead, he took a few deep breaths. He thought, *What the fuck is going on?* Then it dawned on him why he was being harassed. It was June 8, the anniversary of the Burchfield murder. Though by then many guards believed him to be innocent and most were kind—they joked with him, shared stories, even photographs of their children—a few old-timers were still convinced he'd been involved in the murder of their colleague.

The guards had left a bottle of cleaning fluid and some old rags. Jarvis tied a shirt around his mouth and nose to block the smell and set to work. As he scrubbed the walls, floor, toilet—everything—he thought about the fact that after all these years, people like those guards still believed he was a murderer. His anger turned to sadness. He thought back to the trial and saw the Burchfield family sitting in the courtroom. He remembered how badly he wanted to offer his condolences but knew the last thing they wanted was to hear from him. He also thought about the fact that Burchfield's family weren't the only ones impacted. All the COs were—and so were their families. Besides mourning their colleague, they must have been unnerved by such a forceful reminder of how dangerous their jobs were. Any one of them could be the next victim of a prisoner's plot. As Jarvis cleaned, he thought about the enduring grief and fear caused by that single violent act. When the cell was immaculate, he sat in meditation for an hour, and then he slept.

A few days later, Jarvis went out on the yard again and saw Freddie looking good. His eyes were clear, and his smile was bright. When Jarvis asked how he was doing, his old friend reported that he was great, sober. "Practicing those steps," he said. "Meditating in the morning. Doing all this shit. Like you told me."

Freddie asked where Jarvis had been, and he told him what had happened: being moved to the repulsive cell. Freddie knew that Jarvis had paid a very high price over the years for being the only one on death row living in the scene of the crime for which he'd been convicted. Freddie said, "Those motherfuckers," and he went off on the injustice, the sickness of San Quentin, the evil assholes who controlled every aspect of their lives.

In the midst of his rant, Freddie noticed Jarvis's expression. It wasn't the righteous anger he'd expected. His friend's eyes were lit up as though he'd found gold. Jarvis pointed to the ground, leaned over, and picked up a leaf.

He held it up for Freddie to see and said, "Look at this, man, look how beautiful."

Caught in the sunlight, the leaf seemed to glow.

Freddie marveled, *The smallest things Jarvis makes the biggest thing over, and the biggest things he sees as nothing at all.*

WARRIOR

Jarvis had come far during his nearly three decades in San Quentin. When he arrived in the prison at the age of nineteen, he'd been a thug—that was the word he used to describe himself.

Pema hadn't known him during his "thug" years, but she'd seen remarkable changes in him since they met.

Pema recognized that in a place where survival itself was a daily challenge, finding ways to help others was miraculous. Indeed, she described Jarvis as a miracle worker. One day she told him about the concept of the bodhisattva, evoking the powerful image of a "bodhisattva warrior."

A warrior? Jarvis remembered when he thought of himself as a warrior—a warrior in the BGF's revolution. But what was a bodhisattva warrior? He asked her to explain. At its essence, Pema said, it's someone who "connects completely" with human suffering and tries to help people. She said it was extraordinary that he'd found ways to help people in prison, especially on death row.

Then she asked if Jarvis felt ready to take the vows that would affirm the progress he'd made as a warrior for Buddhism. She explained the difference between these vows and the ones he'd made in the ceremony with Rinpoche Chagdud Tulku when he became a Buddhist. "You made a deep and pure commitment to pursue the path to awakening," as Pema described it. "The vows you took then were a commitment to Buddhist practice—we take refuge in the Buddha as a role model of a very courageous person. At a deeper level, it means that when things get difficult, we take refuge in our own Buddha nature, our own good hearts and open minds. We stay present. We practice.

"The bodhisattva vows are the next stage, a natural extension of the initial commitment to Buddhism. Recognizing suffering— living fully in it, unguarded—compels us to prevent it or reduce it when we can. When we set out to support other beings, when we go so far as to stand in their shoes, when we aspire to keep an open heart even when we want to close down—that's a warrior in Buddhism." She said, "It's basically helping—helping even when we find ourselves in uncomfortable waters, which normally makes people run. Talk about moving in uncomfortable waters! Look at where you live!"

Pema asked Jarvis if he remembered when he said he didn't think he could fulfill those vows in prison. "You didn't think you could, but you've found many ways to help. You've helped people who read your book, wrote you, and asked for guidance. You've helped prisoners and guards. Those are all the actions of a Buddhist warrior."

When Jarvis still seemed dubious about his capacity to be a warrior for Buddhism, Pema listed examples of actions he'd taken that showed her he *was* a warrior. She recalled Jarvis's intervention when guards could have been hurt or killed, when he convinced inmates to flood the tier rather than attack them; he'd told the story in *Finding Freedom*. The benefit of the action had gone further than the obvious one that he'd prevented violence and potentially saved lives. He'd also spared inmates the possible repercussions of the violence they'd planned: being beaten, shot with rubber bullets, thrown into solitary.

She also reminded him of the more recent, and more dangerous, occasion when he'd interceded on behalf of the young gay con accused of snitching. As Freddie had said, that intervention had likely saved the young boy's life and could have gotten Jarvis killed.

Pema invoked the first Buddhist parable he'd ever heard, about the Buddha who gave his life to save a mother tiger and her cubs. He'd laughed derisively at it back then, but he'd since become the mother tiger. Then Pema said she'd never heard anyone express the actions of a bodhisattva better than the day he'd told the men on the yard, "The wolves are going to prey on the sheep. We have to protect the sheep."

Jarvis protested, "I don't know where that came from."

"It came from you," Pema said. "You were connecting with your true self, the person you've always been but that was lost inside you. Your heart has opened, and you're discovering your Buddha nature—your true nature."

Two months later, Pema returned to the Bay Area and San Quentin, where she walked along the bay to the East Block visiting hall, which was normally reserved for legal visits. It held two rows of cages. Those along the brick outer wall had windows through which one could glimpse the bay. Pema and Jarvis were locked in a small cage on the parallel row, where the view was a line of vending machines with backlit pictures of cascading waterfalls. Their cage was five by four feet or so, encased in bars covered with sheets of Plexiglas.

Back when Chagdud Tulku conducted the empowerment ceremony, Jarvis had been in the AC, and therefore the ritual was held behind glass, modified for a noncontact visit. Now Jarvis and his teacher could be together in the same space. They hugged and sat in plastic chairs facing each other across a small table. Pema wore her usual robes and Jarvis his prison denim plus a bracelet with polished mala beads—another gift from Pamela.

As Chagdud Tulku had done, Pema had Jarvis repeat prayers. Then she bestowed on him the Buddhist name Sopa Jigme, which means "fearless patience."

Jarvis laughed at that. "Patience? You've gotta be kidding."

She responded, "Well, you've only been in prison for thirty years."

He said, "Okay, I guess. But I'm *not* fearless. You know that."

"Oh, Jigme," she said, "you're as fearless as anyone I know. Anyway, this name is what you have to work on to further awaken—awaken completely. It's what you're uncovering as you go forward toward enlightenment."

When Pema used that word, Jarvis admitted that he'd always found it confusing. He observed that some Buddhists and Buddhist writings talked about the path to enlightenment "as if it was the destination on a road map, and the road goes to the top of a mountain, above the clouds." But, he continued, "That seems to contradict everything I'm learning about Buddhism. You're supposed to be in the middle of suffering, right in the nasty, ugly, filthy swamp, and not turn your back on it."

"That's not enlightenment," Pema explained, "at least not the way I think about it. Yes, enlightenment is often taught as going to the top of the mountain, but then what about all the suffering you've left behind down below? Enlightenment is more like a triangle. You go up one side and reach the top. It doesn't keep going up, it goes down then. It goes down and down right into the pain and the joy experienced by humanity. That's where you find compassion, and that's where enlightenment lies."

She saw that Jarvis still looked uncertain. "Let's say you get to the top of the mountain. You still have your alcoholic brother and schizophrenic mother down at the bottom of the mountain. What about them? There are still people begging on the street for food. What about them? Do you just leave them behind? Is that enlightenment? No," she continued, "the path is going down and down and down into their suffering and the suffering of all the people. You embrace them. You join them. Compassion isn't about looking down on someone who's in worse shape than you and helping the poor person. It's about a relationship between equals. You understand their suffering. You're completely in their shoes. It comes from softening our hearts, opening up to our own and others' pain. To me, that's enlightenment."

The ceremony continued with Pema introducing a form of meditation called *tonglen*, practiced by bodhisattvas. "It can guide your bodhisattva practice." She explained that *tonglen* is breathing in another person's pain and then breathing out what can benefit—comfort or help—them. Then we breathe out healing energy through the air we share with them. "Normally you're told you want to get rid of pain—*breathe out* pain. In this meditation we *take in* others' pain. It's the essential practice of a bodhisattva."

She gave examples. "*Tonglen* can be done for those who are ill or dying—those in pain of any kind. Usually we look away when we see someone suffering. Their pain brings up our fear, anger, and confusion. But when we breathe in their suffering, it blends with our own. It connects with everyone's. Then we breathe out what will help them. The medicine goes from our bodies to them and to everyone through the air we all breathe."

Then she taught Jarvis the four stages of *tonglen* practice: "Rest your mind for a second or two in a state of openness or stillness. Next, begin the visualization. Breathe in feelings of heat, heaviness, and claustrophobia, and breathe out feelings of coolness, brightness, and light. Breathe in completely, taking in negative energy through all the pores of your body. When you breathe out, radiate positive energy through all the pores of your body. Do this until your visualization is synchronized with your in- and out-breaths.

"The next stage is focusing on a painful situation. If you are doing *tonglen* for someone you love, extend it out to all those who are in the same situation. You can do *tonglen* for people close to you and for those you think of as your enemies. Do *tonglen* for them, thinking of them as having the same confusion as your friend. Breathe in their pain, and then send them relief. As you do this practice, gradually, at your own pace, you will be surprised to find yourself more and more able to be there for others."

As the ceremony moved forward, Jarvis sensed a mystifying change in the cage. He'd heard of transmission, which he understood to be a sort of wordless communication between a teacher and a student—Jarvis thought of it as a "mind meld" from *Star Trek*. He'd initially considered it mere Buddhist hocus-pocus, never mind impossible, but as Pema continued, he *felt* her words as much as heard them. He thought, *It's like being plugged into the Matrix, like in the movie, but I'm plugged into Pema's mind.*

Pema talked about the fundamental focus of Buddhism: it always goes back to the suffering of humanity. She might have continued speaking or become silent—it wasn't relevant. In a kind of trance (was this the mind meld?) he went back a long time ago—more than a decade—to the time he'd been meditating and had seen a person, also meditating, in flames. Jarvis had recognized the man as himself. Then he had entered the burning body and experienced the sensation of ascending into the sky and, eventually from space, seeing billions of fires on Earth, each one of them a human in pain.

He'd told Pema about the experience and, guided by her, had the vision again, but there was more this time. He saw himself reaching into one of the fires, grasping the wrist of a burning man, and lifting him out of the flames. He lifted another man out of the flames and then another. In the vision he had a billion arms that reached into a billion fires, each clutching the hands of suffering people inside and pulling them upward. At that moment, he realized he'd spun out into another story, but this wasn't only about suffering; it was an astonishing discovery that his pain had merged with his joy. He breathed and returned to his body. He cried again, as he had the first time he'd had the vision, but these tears were different than ever before. Strangely, they were tears of pain *and* joy—both at once. It was a startling revelation and one that brought a chill: People can simultaneously feel the world's sorrow and the world's joy. He thought, *Is that what they mean when they talk about Nirvana? Is it enlightenment?*

Jarvis became conscious of the cage again—and of holding hands with Pema on top of the table that stood between them. It seemed as if she'd had the same tears he'd had. Then Pema nodded and began meditating, and Jarvis joined her—teacher and student and, more precious in their minds, two friends. A guard tapped on the cage, ending the visit.

*   *   *

Jarvis remained in a dreamlike, almost euphoric state for several days after the ceremony. He chose to stay inside, meditate, and read a biography of Abraham Lincoln. And he wrote.

Writing was still sometimes difficult; he wrestled with words and struggled to get complex ideas onto paper. But when it clicked, it felt extraordinary—a creative burst flowing from his mind through his fingers and onto the page.

One late night, Jarvis began a new story. He'd been struggling to make sense of an experience he'd had with an inmate who'd been in a cell down the tier for six months or so. He knew the man as Bork.* They often talked and played chess.

Generally, men on the row didn't ask one another about their crimes—it was better not to know—but that week Jarvis heard men talking about Bork. One said Bork was on death row because he'd raped and killed children. Jarvis was sickened. He'd been playing chess with a child killer! Even among the killers on death row, cons reserve special enmity for anyone who hurt a child. Over the years, some had been killed. Jarvis felt nausea, disgust, fury, and hatred so intense it consumed him.

Jarvis imagined Bork's victims—the visions were unbearably vivid—and the victims' shattered parents, their wailing grief. He tried to quell his fury with *tonglen* meditation, but it didn't work. In fact, the images only became sharper. So did his anger.

In Jarvis's story, he expressed his repulsion and his failed at-tempts to make peace with the fact that he lived down the tier

*"Bork" is a pseudonym.

from a child killer. "The sound of Bork's voice boot-kicked me further out into the dirty sea of my own pain, where I risked drowning in hatred." He said he felt as if he were living a few cells from Satan. He evoked Red Tara, his protectress, but even she didn't help him comprehend "sickness so deep and absolute that it could cause a human being like Bork to prey upon children." He wrote that it felt "as if I were undergoing spiritual chemotherapy, attached to an intravenous tube that dripped a poisonous substance into my veins."

Jarvis described grappling with the fact that he, supposedly a bodhisattva, wanted to kick someone's teeth in, a desire that shamed him. Then he wrote about what happened next: "As I breathed slowly in and out, absorbed by my anger toward Bork, I saw all the things I didn't want to see. On the screen between my closed eyes, I saw my own anger. I saw the viciousness of my own pain . . . I was ugly, shaken, no good to myself. The structure of my face had changed. All the thin frown lines in my face seemed permanent, and the muscles in my jaw were as tight as clenched fists."

Then "a bigger feeling broke through as I plugged into all the human suffering throughout the world." Jarvis asked himself, "Why hadn't I seen Bork as part of it? Why hadn't I seen myself as part of it. . . . [When I did,] I felt a mental clarity that lifted me above all the clouds of my own making."

* * *

Susan Moon, the *Turning Wheel* editor, suggested that Jarvis collect his recent stories and publish them as a second book. She helped him with rewrites and edits, Pema and Pamela read drafts and offered suggestions, and Rick Targow reviewed the stories to be sure there was nothing in them that would adversely affect his appeal. As the book neared completion, Susan visited one day, and Jarvis asked a guard to allow him to give her a lumpy envelope. Inside was a bouquet he'd made for her using dozens of pen inserts he'd emptied over the previous year.

When the book, entitled *That Bird Has My Wings*, was complete, friends sent early copies to Bishop Desmond Tutu, Sister Helen Prejean, and others, who provided blurbs. (I provided one after reading a manuscript sent by Pamela.) The book was published in September 2009. *Publishers Weekly* described it as a "frank, heartfelt rendering" of Masters's life.

Jarvis was emboldened by the publication of the second book and once again was encouraged by the reaction. As they had after the publication of *Finding Freedom*, letters poured in from people who had been moved by his stories, many of whom shared theirs, including haunting reminders of the infinite sources of suffering, from heartbreak to abuse, loneliness to illness.

Again Jarvis responded to the letters with gratitude, commiseration, and occasionally advice. In a letter that covered fourteen pages, a woman wrote that Jarvis's life reminded her of her own even though she had grown up in relative privilege. "I was abandoned and abused like you," she said. Later in the letter she revealed that she was being abused by her husband. "He loves me, and I love him," she wrote. "He can't help it. My mother doesn't understand. She wants me to leave him. I can't. He needs me." Jarvis responded, "People who are beaten think they deserve it. I did. But we don't deserve it. Violence isn't love. Don't stay with someone who doesn't treat you with the love and respect you deserve." Months later the woman wrote again. She'd taken his advice and felt, for the first time in her life, "free."

In early July, after a visit with Jarvis, Pema departed San Francisco and traveled east to Gampo Abbey, the cliffside monastery in Nova Scotia. Soon after, Jarvis received a letter from Canada in which Pema asked if he wanted to meditate with her on the night of the next full moon. "Midnight your time is 4 a.m. in Nova Scotia," she wrote. "I'll be in retreat in the little cabin. What do you think?"

He responded, "Count on me. I'll be there."

At midnight on the appointed day, Jarvis sat on the floor and repeated a purifying mantra Pema had taught him. Jarvis imagined her sitting in the same pose on the other edge of the continent; she'd sent him postcards with photographs of the abbey, which was set on a desolate promontory overlooking the remote and aptly named Pleasant Bay. He inhaled and began to meditate. He felt her presence; he conceived of it as a long-distance mind meld.

After a few minutes of sitting contentedly, he felt a knot of anxiety in his belly, which began to grow. He had a vision: Pema was looking at him with horror. He began to panic and abruptly ended the meditation. He was breathing hard and felt light-headed, as if he might faint. He breathed deeper in order to steady himself. He was baffled. What happened? He'd been with Pema, after all. His mother.

His mother.

The word hung in his mind. His mother. He realized what had gone wrong. He *had* been connected to Pema. If she felt as connected to him as he did to her, she could see inside him, and that was why he panicked. He so badly wanted to be worthy of Pema's love. His mother's love. He wanted to be a good son. But he *wasn't* good. He didn't want her to see inside him because she'd see the truth.

Pema spent months at a time alone in retreat when she was in Nova Scotia. Though she was secluded in the cabin, the Gampo Abbey staff knew to interrupt her if Jarvis called, which he did the next morning.

"Jarvis!" She was happy to hear his voice. "Good morning! So what did you think?"

Jarvis sounded distressed. "I don't know if you felt it, but I was feeling you there with me, and that was wonderful, Mama, but then something changed."

She asked, "What changed?"

"I was feeling ashamed, like you were seeing the awfulness of what I've done in my past. I was seeing how the harm I've done spreads like a disease. Some really ugly and nasty stuff."

"Jarvis," she said, "you said I saw 'the awfulness' of what you've done. What do you think would happen if I did?"

A lump rose in his throat when he realized the answer: if she saw who he truly was, she'd leave him. As Cynthia had.

Pema didn't wait for him to respond. "Jarvis," she said, "maybe you feel that you don't deserve to be cared for and loved. Over the past few years you've made great strides forgiving others, but what about *you*? Do you think you can forgive *yourself*?"

14

COMPASSION

When he was twelve years old, incarcerated in the juvenile lockup where he was burned with cigarettes, made to fight other boys, and brutally beaten, the staff forced Jarvis and other state wards to take part in "blanket parties." In the middle of the night, they'd surround one of their sleeping friends and bludgeon him with flails made of bars of soap inside pillowcases. The boy would awake screaming. The weapons weren't supposed to leave marks, but they did—they left massive bruises and welts—and once a boy Jarvis liked was rendered unconscious.

In the weeks following the phone call with Pema, when Jarvis meditated on her question—could he forgive himself?—he realized that before he could consider forgiving himself, he had to understand what he had to forgive himself for. When he did, shameful memories like the blanket parties arose. Jarvis told Pema about them and said the memories made him feel furious, afraid, and guilty. He understood feeling angry—he recalled wanting to turn on the counselors and beat *them*—and scared, but why guilty?

Pema responded, "It wasn't your fault, but as a sensitive child, of course you'd feel bad about hurting those boys."

Jarvis countered, "But that's not why I feel guilty. It's not the main reason, anyway. I feel guilty because the whole time I was whooping those boys"—he felt his stomach tighten—"I was glad it was them and not me."

They were quiet, contemplating those words. Then Pema spoke. First she assured him that that reaction was normal, too. Anyone, especially a child, would be glad to escape violence. "But maybe," she added, "you were ready to take on that guilt because you already felt you were a bad person."

Why would a child feel that way? Pema reminded him that all children are predisposed to take as the truth whatever circumstances they encounter—they don't know anything different. For kids who were brutalized, this "truth" includes a belief that they deserve whatever punishment they receive. A child asks himself, *Why was I beaten? Why did they leave me?* And he answers, *Because I'm bad. I got what I deserve.* Pema said, "Children who grow up believing they're bad often commit actions that confirm what they'd been taught about themselves."

"Even if they know better?"

Pema said yes. The wounds of childhood cut deeply. The

psychological damage can override our best instincts, at least until we face those wounds.

Jarvis wasn't ready to let himself off the hook. "But a lot of the cons in here were never taught right from wrong," he said. "I was. They didn't have a choice, but I did. I was taught when I was little. Mamie and Dennis taught me to be kind, think about others, the Golden Rule."

Jarvis explained that his time with the Procks had taught him empathy—he once described Mamie as his first Buddhist teacher— yet he willfully ignored those lessons. He recalled the year he'd spent hitting liquor and grocery stores and fast-food restaurants. He'd made a deal with a boy who worked at a gas station. Wielding a gun he took from an uncle's arsenal, he'd rob the place, and the kid would call the police and misidentify him. It was profitable until Jarvis caught his accomplice skimming money from the heists. He wanted to scare the kid, so he pointed a gun at his head and threatened to kill him. The boy fell to his knees and begged for his life. Jarvis let him go but not before he saw the abject terror in the boy's eyes. Those eyes still haunted him.

He was also haunted by the night he and a friend huffed gasoline and smoked dope and, brandishing shotguns Jarvis "borrowed" from another uncle, entered a Kmart through different doors. His friend fired into the ceiling, and chunks of plaster and dust rained down. Shoppers screamed, parents grabbed their children and dropped to the floor. Many cried. Jarvis had pushed away memories of their faces, too. He'd terrorized them. He'd traumatized them. "I knew better. I knew it when I did those crimes.

"Here's the thing," he continued. "Death row is filled with people who never had a chance to go another way in their lives, but I did. I *could* have gone another way—I'd been taught right from wrong. And here's another thing. I had opportunities a lot of these guys never had, but I didn't take them."

Pema asked, "What opportunities?"

Jarvis told her about his time as a teenager between lockups. To blow off steam, he'd sometimes steal a car and go joyriding. Once he jacked a Monte Carlo and drove north on the freeway, exited on Wilshire, and parked near UCLA. He walked through the campus and sat on a bench, watching students and teachers. They were different from anyone he knew. Most of them were white, but that wasn't the crucial difference. Those people looked as though they were going somewhere; they had purpose.

Jarvis followed a group into a lecture hall and sat in the back while the professor talked. Sitting in the class, he heard a voice in his head telling him to learn, to find a different life. He could go to college, too. He could be one of those students.

He returned to the campus a few times and sat in on other classes. He even carried a fake textbook he'd made from a phone book so no one would know he was an imposter. But *he* knew he was an imposter. "I knew the truth. I wasn't one of those kids and never would be. College wasn't going to happen for me. I felt stupid— *embarrassed*—for thinking it could."

He drew a breath and continued, "But when I got older, I had a chance to go to college. I did. I came real close. I could have had a completely different life."

Jarvis had never shared anything about his opportunity to go to college with Pema before. After moving out of the juvenile justice system, he was placed in the state's Youth Authority. Beginning when he was sixteen, judges sent him to a series of YA institutions. One was O. H. Close, a lockup in Stockton. His first day there, he got into a fight and counselors were taking him to an isolation wing, where beatings and solitary confinement awaited him. But on the way, a counselor—Jarvis remembered him clearly, Hershey Johnson—stopped him, took him to another room, sat him down in front of a TV set, and switched it on to some cartoons. He sat down at a desk to do paperwork and left Jarvis watching *Tom and Jerry*, *The Flintstones*, and *The Jetsons*. Jarvis forgot where he was and started laughing, then looked up and saw Hershey watching him. He felt caught. "Like he caught me being what I was, which was a little kid pretending to be a man. I was swearing and fighting, pushing people and stealing from them—but that wasn't me. I wasn't mean. I was acting mean. I wasn't violent. I was acting violent. Hershey came over and said, 'Jarvis, you don't have to be what everybody's telling you you have to be.'"

Those words stayed with him. He stopped acting out, and for the first time in any institution, he participated eagerly in programs, group therapy, and classes. A few months later, Hershey told Jarvis he only needed a couple more classes to graduate high school. Jarvis didn't understand how that was possible. He'd been kicked out of two schools and had hardly attended classes since then, but the institutions were required by the state to keep the kids on track in school. It hadn't done so, but it had given him credit for courses he'd never taken. He thought, *What the hell?*, took a few more courses—photography, acting, writing—and got a diploma embossed with a gold stamp.

In 1979, at seventeen, Jarvis had a high school diploma, no write-ups, and an exit report from YA in which a counselor had written that he was qualified to become a trainee at a solar energy company—or to attend college. "I remember Hershey saying 'You're smart as hell and talented,' and he encouraged me to go."

"And?" Pema asked. "Then what happened?"

After graduation, Jarvis moved into a group home founded by a retired basketball player to help kids transition out of the juvenile criminal justice system. He had a girlfriend, and he was thinking about starting college in the fall. In the meantime, he worked as a busboy.

Then one Sunday afternoon, the phone rang in the group home. His mother was calling from Harbor City. She'd been in the hospital, but she was out, she was clean, and she wanted him home. She said his sisters were out of foster care and home, too—the family was all together, except for him. Cynthia said, "You get down here."

"Hershey warned me not to go to LA. And I knew myself that it would be a mistake to go back. But that didn't stop me. I got home, went out and robbed a gas station. Cops picked me up, and the judge sent me back north to another YA jail, but I hopped a fence with a friend and went back down to LA. I started robbing everything in sight. I was arrested, and that was the last time I was free. A lifetime ago."

He continued, "See, I *did* have a choice. I could have gone to college and had a different life. I had options; I could have gone another way, but here I am. How do I forgive myself for that?"

Revealing all that to Pema made him face it himself as he never had before, and regret weighed down on him. But he pressed on, admitting what he believed to be the ultimate self-betrayal because it put him on death row. "Back when I was charged with taking part in Sergeant Burchfield's murder, I didn't defend myself by telling what had really happened: I wasn't part of any conspiracy, didn't know it was going to happen, didn't make the knife," he said. "But I'd taken the oath, and I was loyal to it. I didn't talk. But I think about why they chose me to be the fall guy. I was chosen because the con who set me up knew I'd follow orders, wouldn't say a word. I was a good soldier and lived the code, no matter the consequences." He concluded, "My weakness put me on death row. How do I forgive myself for that?"

Pema let those words hang in the air for a moment before she spoke. "Some of our experiences have an enduring impact," she said. "We may never fully get over them. But we can reframe them."

She reminded him of *tonglen* meditation and explained more about it. "*Tonglen* isn't only breathing in others' pain. It's also breathing in our *own* pain. We breathe it in and then breathe out what we need to heal. You beat yourself up because you feel you deserve it. Maybe you didn't go to college because you felt you didn't deserve a better life. Maybe you went home to Harbor City because you felt you didn't deserve a better life. Maybe you didn't listen to your conscience because you'd never learned how to—you'd already been convinced you weren't any good.

"Breathe in all that pain, Jarvis. Breathe it all in. Then breathe out what you need. Here's the magic of *tonglen*. You'll begin breathing in your own pain, but you'll soon realize you're breathing in everyone's pain. Then, after you breathe in all that poison, you're breathing out into the world—to every person. You're breathing out what you need and what everyone needs. What do you need? What does everyone need? Compassion, caring, and love."

Again invoking Judge Savitt's cruel words when she handed down Jarvis's death sentence, Pema added, "The judge said the world would have been a better place if you'd never been born. Breathe that pain in. Then breathe out a message for you and everyone: the world is a better place *because* you were born."

In the middle of that year, Jarvis was moved to another cell—once again without explanation. It was next door to an old acquaintance. A decade earlier, Jarvis was celled next to a con named Richard Roberts.* They rarely saw each other face-to-face, but they talked on the yard and through the wall they shared.

The vagaries of prison bureaucracy made them neighbors again, and they quickly renewed their bond. Roberts was married and had two children. For more than ten years, his wife had written letters every week or two and sent photos of the kids. Using a fishline, Roberts sent snapshots to Jarvis, who teased him, "They're lucky they got their mother's looks."

A half year later, Roberts complained that his wife hadn't visited

*"Richard Roberts" is a pseudonym.

or written in a month. There was still no word a month later, when Jarvis began noticing Roberts's speech slurring. When he asked if everything was all right, his neighbor said he was fine, just high, admitting he'd gotten ahold of some pain pills.

The next morning at four o'clock, Jarvis heard chaos on the tier. Guards rushed by his cell and stopped at Roberts's.

Jarvis heard a guard yell, "He's unconscious."

Guards carried Roberts's body out of his cell and placed it on a gurney parked directly in front of Jarvis's cell. Jarvis stared at the man on the gurney whom he'd known for years but had rarely seen. One of the guards began pumping his chest with the heels of his hands, but there was no response. The guard didn't stop. Jarvis recognized the CO. He had a reputation for brutality, and over the years Jarvis had been one of the targets of his cruelty.

As Jarvis watched, the guard worked feverishly to revive Roberts, but his work was in vain. He bent down and put his ear near Roberts's mouth. Then he placed two fingers gently on Roberts's neck.

At last, the guard said quietly, "He's gone."

The guard looked up and saw Jarvis staring at him. Both men were nearly crying.

It was risky for Jarvis to say anything—he didn't know if the volatile guard would lash out—but he addressed the cop. "Thanks for trying."

Jarvis said it again. "Thanks for trying to save him."

The guard studied Jarvis. He said nothing, but his look revealed his bewilderment, and then he averted his eyes.

Jarvis was left with sorrow over his neighbor's death but also something incongruous and disorienting. Though he'd known the guard for years, he hadn't seen him as a person until that morning.

When Pema next visited, she saw in Jarvis's eyes and heard in the words that tumbled out that something momentous had happened. He told her about Roberts's suicide, how heartbroken he was. Then he spoke about the many suicides since he'd been on death row. They were so common that guards and prisoners usually took them in stride. He'd hear a guard's voice: "We've got a hanger." They cut him down, his body was taken away, and everything went on as normal.

"A 'hanger,'" Jarvis said sadly. "Like in the Billie Holiday song: 'Strange fruit hanging from the poplar trees.' Not a person. No name."

Jarvis told Pema about the guard's effort to save Roberts and the moment they locked eyes. "I've lived with cops all my life," he said. "They were the enemy. It was 'us'—my family, neighbors, all of us growing up, every con—and 'them'—police."

Enmity between guards and inmates ran deep, and it was mutual. "If I looked in a cop's eyes, I saw hate," Jarvis said. "Now"—he paused for a moment—"I think about them differently. Look at them, really look at them, and you see pain. They're just like cons in that way. We're the same—they suffer, too."

Jarvis continued, "So yeah, some are SOBs, but maybe they're the ones who've gone through the most hell. Some of them probably want to do good, but . . . I was thinking how it must make them feel to work all day in a place where they're hated. They're prisoners, too."

After a minute Jarvis said, "All those years ago Rinpoche told me I should learn to see the perfection of all beings, which I didn't understand. What the fuck was that? But now I understand."

At times like that, when conversations with Pema helped clarify his thinking, Jarvis felt physically lighter. He told her, "It takes a lot of energy to carry hate. Letting it go . . . I feel . . ." He searched for the word and then found it: ". . . liberated."

15

WALKING ON THE GRASS

Back in February 2007, just before the bodhisattva ceremony and the publication of his book, Jarvis had heard from Joe Baxter that the California Supreme Court had ordered an evidentiary hearing at which a judge would review some of the claims in Jarvis's appeals. It was the Valentine's gift he and Marie celebrated. Jarvis had been waiting for his appeals to be heard since 2001, when Baxter and the other lawyers filed the initial papers. He and Marie were ecstatic, but they hadn't known it would take another three years for the hearing to be scheduled.

As the date of the hearing approached and the stakes sank in, Jarvis's fear mounted. Sometimes he imagined winning and leaving the prison, and his heart pounded so hard he thought it might induce another seizure. As scary as that was, though, when he imagined losing, he felt as if his heart would stop and he'd die.

All he'd wanted was for his case to be heard—a chance to prove his innocence—but now that the actual court date was approaching, he felt panic.

Pema recognized his distress and counseled him to focus on his practice. "Try your best to stay in the middle," she said, "not to spin out on outcomes you can't predict or control, either positive or negative. Don't deny the hope and fear; let yourself feel them both. But work with your breath to stay in the middle. Hope and fear are two sides of the same coin. Both are traps. But remember how both rob you of the present moment. Your practice will help you get through this."

The hearing finally commenced in January 2011. Jarvis made daily trips to the courthouse, where he sat at the table next to his lawyers, shackled except for his left hand, which was kept uncuffed so he could take notes. The room brought unnerving memories of the earlier trial: same courtroom, same buzzing fluorescent lights, a new judge who'd grant him a new trial or send him back to death row.

Jarvis had been convicted and sentenced in Marin County Superior Court. In order to resolve factual issues that his attorneys had raised in their direct appeal and habeas corpus filings, the state supreme court ordered the county to respond to seven questions related to the charge that Jarvis had been convicted on false evidence, and whether there was new evidence of his innocence. Jarvis had reason to be optimistic because the court's "order to show cause" was, as Baxter told the *San Francisco Chronicle*, "unique and breathtaking in its scope."

Marie tried not to get overly confident or excited, but she quietly began to plan his homecoming. *He had to win. Of course he'd win.*

Jarvis tried his best to follow Pema's instructions. He used meditation techniques, focusing on his breath, to stay as even as he could. His mind often spun out, though, and he swung from terror to hope and back again. Then the pause would come. When he recognized it, he pulled himself out of the turmoil back into his body, but it was hard to do, especially as the hearing progressed, and once again he had to listen to the prosecution portray him as it had in the original trial, as a cold-blooded killer, unrepentant and irredeemable. Sometimes he felt scared and sometimes enraged. He inhaled. He tried to focus on the in-breath and the air in his lungs. On his breath leaving his body. Slowly. He breathed. It helped for moments at a time, but he wasn't adept enough to breathe that fury away—or that fear.

Even in his state of turmoil, Jarvis was aware of a significant difference between the original murder trial and this one. Last time he had been alone except for Melody, Kelly Hayden, and their families. This time when he looked over his shoulder, he saw their loving faces and many others, too. Alan Senauke was busy taking notes, chronicling the trial on his blog. Marie, Pamela, Susan, and others were there. He had support he hadn't had last time, and his friends' presence provided some comfort.

One Saturday, Pamela visited, and they spent an hour laughing—for a while he forgot about the hearing. When they did talk about the case, Jarvis admitted how stressful it was, but he was philosophical. He spoke as much to himself as to her. "I just have to keep reminding myself that thoughts about the future lead to torment, but when I'm in the moment—like now, here, with you"—he gazed at Pamela; her once flaming red hair had silvered, but her honey-brown eyes shone as brightly as ever—"I'm okay."

Marie visited, too, but those meetings were more somber. They didn't talk much; they didn't need to. They shared each other's anticipation and fear.

Evenings after court and on weekends, Jarvis spoke to Pema. As she heard his apprehension intensify, she reassured him that it was natural for him to worry. "At times like this, our minds can go to very dark places," she said. "Don't deny those thoughts, acknowledge them, and then return to your breath." He tried his best but was in a tailspin. One night he wrote Pema a letter: "The other day, meditating, I felt something, like I was holding it like a hot potato that was burning my hands. I looked up and was seeing my executioners, their silence, going through what was a routine for them, like holding me down, tying straps around me. I tried faking like I had this compassion for them while they held me down. I was trying to accept that I was dying and it was time to let go. I didn't want to let go, Pema. I do not want to let go."

The grounds for Jarvis's appeals included evidence of prosecutorial misconduct and the recantations of key witnesses. In a posttrial statement, a star witness claimed that a prosecutor had refused to move him to another prison unless he cooperated. Because he'd been exposed as a known informer, if the inmate wasn't transferred he'd probably have been killed. Another witness said he'd been advised not to disclose a prosecutor's promise of leniency in another case. Most significantly, a prisoner had confessed to a corrections officer that he'd committed the crimes for which Jarvis had been convicted but Jarvis's defense had been denied the right to present the confession.

Some of the most damning evidence used against Jarvis consisted of kites he'd written after the murder. Jarvis's lawyers believed the prosecution had determined that the testimony of snitches wasn't enough to convict Jarvis, and it coerced a BGF member to force Jarvis, under threat, to copy two kites in which he implicated himself. A forensic linguist who'd studied hundreds of pages of Jarvis's writing testified that Jarvis had indeed copied the kites (which he'd never contested) but hadn't composed them. He'd been forced to copy them, or he could have been killed. An expert in gang culture explained that gang leaders often forced young soldiers like Jarvis to take dictation and copy kites and other documents, after which the originals were destroyed so there'd never be incriminating communications in their own handwriting.

Jarvis's friends believed that the evidence was incontrovertible. Kelly said it was a "slam dunk." She believed the court couldn't help but see that he was innocent and the trial had been a sham. Their confidence heightened his, and his anxiety increased as he spun more stories in which he walked out the San Quentin gates.

* * *

The decision handed down on August 22, 2011, was a brutal blow. The judge was unconvinced by Jarvis's lawyers' arguments. She concluded that false evidence had been presented at Jarvis's trial but didn't believe it would have made a difference in the outcome. She discounted the testimony of recanting witnesses whom she found "utterly lacking in credibility" as "career criminals whose word, under oath or otherwise, means nothing." She said their recantations were no more believable than their trial testimony but didn't address the contradiction inherent in that conclusion. If the witnesses were liars and their testimony was unreliable, why would she assume they had been more credible in the late 1980s when prosecutors and the district attorney had made deals with them?

Jarvis's supporters were outraged and distraught. Marie was heartbroken. In tears, she told Pamela, "I just want my husband to come home." She and Pamela cried together.

Jarvis felt broken. He tried to exercise but couldn't. He wrote, but his stories went nowhere, and he was too demoralized to meditate. He was despondent for weeks. During that period a visiting monk pointed out that Jarvis's reaction "wasn't very Buddhist."

Jarvis replied, "Fuck you."

When she heard about his response to the monk, Pema laughed and told him it was exactly the right reaction. The Buddha couldn't have said it better himself.

That moment of laughter shifted something, and that night Jarvis lay on his bunk, still despairing until, around two or three in the morning, he drifted off to sleep. The respite was short lived, because he awoke gasping like a person drowning who, after frantically paddling upward, reaches the surface. The swallow of oxygen felt cleansing. He felt released from a months-long delusion in which he'd succumbed to what Pema called *shenpa*, the Buddhist concept of "attachment," which she translated as "getting hooked" on an idea, fantasy, person, drug, or anything else that preoccupies us. Encouraged by Jarvis's well-meaning friends and dreaming with Marie of their life together, he'd gotten hooked on the fantasy of being freed from San Quentin. In the process, he left behind his practice and himself.

Jarvis moved from his bunk to the floor. He sat in the lotus position, closed his eyes, and breathed. He fell into a deep meditative state for the first time in months and felt . . . what was it? By then he knew that a Buddhist's feelings are never simple or singular. He teased apart what he was experiencing. He felt a blend of sorrow over the loss in court but also relief and a sense of safety. The relief was from being released from the story in which he'd been trapped. The safety was being back in his own mind and body.

The next morning, Jarvis called Kelly, who commiserated and reminded him that the most important stage of his appeal, the habeas corpus stage, was coming, and in that round the court would hear evidence gathered since the original trial.

Jarvis interrupted her. "Guess what?" he said. "I never told you. So every morning on the way to court and every afternoon after court, the guards led me to and from the prison van on this winding sidewalk that cut through this huge green grassy lawn.

"The last day, in spite of the guards and chains, I pushed to the edge of the sidewalk and stepped off. I took one, two, three steps before they yanked me back on the concrete."

Kelly waited to see where the story was going. When Jarvis realized she hadn't gotten it, he said, "Kelly! Don't you see? I walked on the grass!"

She responded, "You got some *grass?*"

He laughed hard. "No," he said. "I *walked* on grass. It was the first time in thirty years I walked on grass!"

Jarvis reveled in the memory of the feeling of the crush of grass beneath his feet. After the call, he saw a truth about Buddhism that he'd never seen so plainly before: the measure of a Buddhist's progress isn't how a person avoids falling, because falls are inevitable; the true measure is how they bounce back.

16

PRESENCE

A year later, on February 24, 2012, Jarvis turned fifty years old. On his half-century birthday, he contemplated the fact that he'd been in San Quentin since he was nineteen—that is, for thirty years, ten years longer than he'd been on the outside. Five years earlier, when he'd been moved from the AC to East Block, a guard brought Jarvis a box of personal property the prison had held since his death sentence, possessions prohibited in the Adjustment Center. It included clothes that had been in storage for two decades. He tried on a jacket and pair of pants, but the sleeves and pant legs were too short. He realized that at the time of the trial he wasn't fully grown. He'd been only a boy.

Nine months after his birthday, San Quentin chaplain Father

George Williams stopped by Jarvis's cell and said he wanted to introduce him to someone, an interfaith minister named Susan Shannon who'd been teaching general-population inmates classes in meditation and restorative justice. She was a Buddhist who'd taken her empowerment vows in a ceremony conducted by the Dalai Lama, and—he saved this tidbit for last—had been taught by Chagdud Tulku Rinpoche, who had given them both their Red Tara initiations.

Susan hadn't ever been to death row and was nervous the morning Father George took her to meet Jarvis. She was made to "vest up"—don a stab-proof vest—before being led down the tier. Their first moments together unsettled her. Looking through the double-diamond wire mesh into Jarvis's cell, she felt Rinpoche's "grace." She and Jarvis quickly fell into an intense conversation about their teacher. The more they talked about his practice and what Buddhism meant to him—how he'd survived because of it—the more intensely she felt that Chagdud Tulku was on the tier with them.

Susan said she believed Rinpoche would have loved that two of his students were meeting—and even more that they were meeting on death row. Jarvis agreed. "He's rubbing his hands up there, thinking, 'Ah, this ought to be good.'"

Susan asked what it had been like when Chagdud Tulku visited him.

"You should have seen the looks he got in the visiting hall," Jarvis said. "These cats never seen anything like him. Like he was dropped in from the moon."

There was time for only a quick conversation that day. Before Susan and Father George left, he suggested that she and Jarvis might want to meet regularly and study together, and so over the weeks that followed they held a sort of private Buddhist study group at the door of his cell. Some of their talks were lighthearted, about their lives. Susan told Jarvis about her evolution to Buddhism, her family, and her beloved horse stabled in West Marin. He reminisced about Harbor City and talked about the challenges he'd faced when he tried to apply Buddhist principles on death row.

Jarvis began to see Susan as a teacher with whom he could study more formal aspects of the religion. He prepared for their meetings with lists of questions. He asked about the many different forms of Buddhism, about the Buddha himself, and the meaning of mantras he'd been taught. Susan taught him the Sanskrit and Tibetan alphabets, and he memorized line by line the Red Tara prayer in the original Tibetan.

Jarvis asked more about Red Tara. He asked why their teacher chose to offer him the protection of a Buddha in the female rather than the traditional male form. Susan explained that Red Tara was one of their teacher's central practices, and she could be equated with Mother Mary and the qualities of what she described as the "Divine Feminine," virtues such as nurturing and empathy. "Do you think a place like San Quentin, where there are thousands of suffering men, might benefit from the protection of a loving mother?"

"At first I thought of Red Tara as some being coming down from the sky like a superhero," Jarvis said, "but Rinpoche made me understand she protects in a different way, almost like covering me over with a blanket—kind of an invisibility cloak."

Jarvis recalled the first time Chagdud Tulku told him that Red

Tara was a force he could summon when he needed help, and he remembered times he *had* needed her and called, and she came and did help. He also remembered times he'd called and she hadn't come—when he was in despair about the evidentiary hearing and again during the months he spent enraged about Bork, for example. Susan explained that Tara doesn't magically take worries away but protects us while we face them.

After a few weeks, Father George arranged for Susan and Jarvis to meet together in a room reserved for psychiatric visits. Sitting at a table in a small room adorned with a poster of a puppy, they talked about reincarnation, mindfulness, and karma, and she taught him more about Buddhist texts. Jarvis shared stories about how his practice played out every day in prison.

The more Susan got to know Jarvis, the more clearly she saw the sincerity with which he practiced his vows. She saw how he extended himself to help people. He told her about a mantra he'd created that he repeated to himself throughout the day. He used the mantra—"How can I be helpful? How can I be helpful?"—to guide him. "When I'm drifting off into some worry, the question brings me back where I need to be."

Jarvis said he'd been trying to find new ways to help others in San Quentin. He'd long fantasized about getting out of prison and working with gangs and teaching kids to meditate, though he wouldn't call it that, because no one would come. He'd open a boxing or martial arts gym, where he'd teach body-mind awareness, "centering"—sitting, breathing—and lessons of Buddhism repackaged for the hood. He'd guide kids to value themselves and live authentically, with the aim of helping them avoid gangs, drugs, and violence. He thought about the question he'd had to face once: Who are you without those homeboys? He wanted to help kids find out. He wanted to let boys know that being a genuine man wasn't the kind of manhood they'd been taught. It wasn't being hard and violent but conscientious, open, and caring.

As long as he was in prison, that plan was on hold. In the meantime, he wanted to find ways he could help men like he'd been helped, and he asked Susan if she had ideas.

Ever since it had been published, well-worn copies of *Finding Freedom* had circulated on death row. Some cons who'd read the book had asked Jarvis to explain more about his practice, and several asked if it could help them. He told the men about Buddhism's views on suffering, death, and living in the present, and he recommended books, including Pema's, Chagdud Tulku's, and a Buddhist book written for prisoners, *We're All Doing Time*, whose author, Bo Lozoff, had visited him. He even taught some cons to meditate.

Jarvis found that some men read the books, some pursued Buddhism, and some tried meditation, but most of them didn't follow through on their initial impulse to take up the faith. Some who tried found it too difficult and stopped. Some who read the books put them aside, finding them obscure and, as one said, "full of guru shit." Jarvis asked Susan, "How can I help more people inside like Buddhism is helping me?"

"Maybe at first they don't need to grasp the practices and ideals at all," she suggested. "They can benefit if they rely on your presence."

"My presence?" Jarvis didn't understand.

She explained, "You have cultivated a presence here on death row that they feel, or they wouldn't be asking. It's thanks to Chagdud's grace, but also to your diligence in your practice." She explained that the *tonglen* and Red Tara practices can create a presence that is palpable to people. "Your neighbors probably feel that from you, though they might not be able to put their fingers on it. Allowing them to spend time with that feeling might be a start of their own transformation. Model it. Practice. If they observed you and have asked, it's because they see something in you. Or feel it. Maybe peacefulness. Maybe wisdom. They sense you have something that could help them."

Susan assured him that more opportunities to help would present themselves. "Sometimes it might mean just listening to a person's struggles and confusion," she said. "You might find opportunities to talk with men and ask them to think about what they are missing in their lives and what qualities they would like to acquire. Maybe you can help them identify their intentions. You can talk about ways they can get to where they want to go and the obstacles in their way to getting there. Maybe eventually they'll try meditation if they see it as a way to open their mind and lead them to the answers they're looking for. Given where they come from and where they live, it wouldn't be a surprise if they seek a way to quiet their minds. You can offer that."

She concluded, "The main thing is keep your mantra going, and you'll get answers. You'll find there are limitless ways to help—and a limitless need for help."

*   *   *

As if to confirm Susan's prediction, an opportunity to help presented itself later that week. Jarvis was on the yard when he noticed a new arrival—a skinny kid, maybe twenty-five, who stood alone, leaning against the fence. He saw through the boy's attempt at projecting menace: the taut jaw, the clenched fists. He'd been that boy.

Jarvis approached the kid, introduced himself, and asked what was up. The boy glared and said, "Fuck off," which made Jarvis smile.

Jarvis didn't push, but he kept his eye on the youngster to be sure he stayed safe. A week or so later, he got the kid talking. He learned his name was Reggie,* he was from Fresno, and he'd killed a teenage boy in a shoot-out between rival gangs.

Reggie's death sentence was fresh, and Jarvis saw that it hadn't yet sunk in. Jarvis told the boy about himself—his family, his neighborhood—and asked about Reggie's. The details were different but, in its essence, Reggie's life was his. The boy hardly knew his father, and his mother had been addicted and violent.

Jarvis reminisced about Cynthia. "She was a gangster," he said, "would cut your damn throat if you got in her way. She carried a box cutter. Once she was attacked and beaten, shot seven times and left in an alley. She didn't die—they couldn't kill her. She was in the hospital for three months. I played on the hospital bed and she told me stories. She was there when I was arrested. She jumped on police, attacked them. She would do anything for her children." He

*"Reggie" is a pseudonym.

stopped to reflect and then said: "But yeah, she hurt us, too. She didn't protect us."

Jarvis told Reggie about his struggle to reconcile his love for a woman who'd inflicted so much pain, how his years in prison—and Buddhism itself—had helped him understand her. "She'd suffered like I did," Jarvis said. "She had that pain. That's what Buddhism teaches: We all have that pain. I began to feel sorry for her. She couldn't help doing what she did. I realized we were the same. My love for her was buried under my hate."

Reggie was spellbound. It was apparent that he was ready to cry, but he wasn't going to let himself.

"See," Jarvis continued, "Buddhism is about how we're all the same, in this world together, struggling. Life is hard for everyone— we're all suffering together." Then he added, "And it shows us how we cause so much of our own suffering."

Jarvis quoted one of the most profound lessons from Buddhism that helped him when he was Reggie's age: "I learned we can control our minds." He let those words settle for a moment. "The trick is to learn how to control them. When we do, our suffering lessens. That's what Buddhism's all about."

When Reggie said, "But I could never be a Buddhist," Jarvis responded, "The thing is, you *are* a Buddhist." He explained, "People think it's Buddha saying 'Sit down, wake up, pray, find a robe, shave your head, empty the mind.' It's not like that. It is that you can take in the thoughts—the bad thoughts—the good ones, too. You can sit with them. You practice, and you realize if you don't run from your fears, your doubts, your past—whatever hurts you—when you face them, they stop chasing you. It changes how you feel about yourself, your life, even here. Buddhism also changes how you react to events. So if you stop running, face your shit . . . That's how you'll keep your young ass out of trouble."

Jarvis concluded by quoting the teacher whose words had helped him at the start of his own journey, George Clinton: "Free your mind and your ass will follow." He said, "Try it. Practice. You'll see if it helps you."

Reggie tried meditating a few times and reported his experiences to Jarvis. He felt moments of peace, but, as Jarvis had, he often became discouraged. Once he said, "This is all fucked up, it's a fucking waste of time. Buddhism is horseshit."

Jarvis responded, "It might be, but even if it is, it can help you get through these hard nights." Then Jarvis asked, "What do you have to lose? You're on death row! That's what I realized when I didn't want to do this stuff. I found out that having nothing to lose frees you up."

He described Pema's concept of groundlessness and said, "When you're in hell and things can't get any worse, you can try things you never tried before. Like trusting people. Looking at yourself. Admitting you're scared."

When Jarvis said that, he felt Rinpoche inside him again.

Jarvis coached Reggie for a year, until the boy was moved to a new yard. After that he sent him books and messages. Reggie sent kites asking questions and describing breakthroughs. In one kite he wrote, "I was meditating and became this bird. I was flying. I realized I was flying in the sky and could go wherever I wanted to go."

17

THE SOUND OF LIFE

Years ago, Jarvis told Pema he wished he could start a class in meditation and Buddhism on death row. He'd once believed that Buddhism was irrelevant in prison but had come to believe it could help every inmate. They lived in hell, and Buddhism taught practitioners to find peace and meaning wherever they were. Peace waited where there was no past or future, and meditation was the path to that place.

Jarvis often thought of a parable Pema once told him: A woman walking in the forest comes upon a pride of tigers. (Jarvis joked, "In Buddhism, tigers are always around teaching stuff.") The tigers begin chasing her and she runs. They're getting closer when she comes to a cliff. There are vines growing down and, holding on to them, she descends. But then she looks below her and sees more tigers waiting at the bottom of the cliff. She looks again and sees a mouse above her gnawing at the vines. When she looks straight ahead, she sees beautiful ripe strawberries growing in front of her. She looks up and sees the tigers, looks down and sees more tigers, and looks above her and sees the mouse chewing the vine onto which she clings. Then she takes a strawberry and savors it.

In her book *Wisdom of No Escape and the Path of Loving Kindness*, Pema says the parable describes "the predicament we're always in, in terms of our birth and death." She writes, "Tigers above, tigers below. . . . Each moment is just what it is. It might be the only moment of our life; it might be the only strawberries we'll ever eat. We could get depressed about it, or we could finally appreciate it and delight in the preciousness of every single moment of life."

Jarvis saw that the "live in and appreciate the present moment" teaching of Buddhism was a profound lesson for anyone, but potentially lifesaving for prisoners. Chagdud Tulku had said, "We're all in prison, and we all have the key." When Jarvis first heard the aphorism, he'd been cynical, even angry. *I don't hold the keys to my chains and cells; my keepers do.* But when he became a Buddhist, he learned it was true. When his mind was free, he was free. Prison walls disappeared. Reggie experienced it, and he wanted other prisoners to experience it, too. He wanted them to know they could find freedom no matter where they dwelled.

Jarvis tested ways to spread the Buddhist message without

mentioning the religion. He wasn't ever going to be one of those born-again proselytizers who turned people off and pissed them off (they'd always pissed *him* off). Jarvis had watched Freddie's growing embrace of Buddhism, and his unique methods of disseminating the teachings. It amused him when he listened in to Freddie on the yard one day talking to a young con about Buddhism as if he were a scholar. Then Freddie told the terrified boy, "If you don't fucking sit there and breathe, don't bother coming out on this yard."

Jarvis's tactics were more subtle. He surveyed the yard and noticed men who seemed isolated. He approached them and got them talking if he could, and he listened to them. He tried to find small ways to help them. "I'm here if you need anything." "It doesn't help to be pissed off at that guard. You'll just get yourself in trouble. Just breathe, man. Just breathe." When a con seemed open to it, he suggested meditation. "I wouldn't have survived in here without it. It's a way to get out of here for a while."

As Jarvis found ways to teach some of the lessons of Buddhism without mentioning its name, some men, like Reggie and Freddie, wanted to learn about the religion itself, and Jarvis believed a Buddhist class on death row would help them. At San Quentin, depending on their sentence and records, general-population inmates could participate in a variety of programs, including college, restorative-justice training, and courses in financial literacy and "positive parenting." However, death row inmates weren't eligible for most of these programs. Before Susan Shannon, it had been impossible for Jarvis to start a Buddhist class because the prison administration wouldn't have allowed it, but because of Susan's official status as a prison chaplain, she could create one. From their first meeting, Susan believed that Chagdud Tulku Rinpoche had brought her and Jarvis together for a purpose. She'd asked Jarvis, "What does our lama want of us?" Here was an answer.

Susan spoke with Father George, and he made arrangements.

San Quentin had a cavernous chapel that was used by the general population. Christian, Jewish, and Muslim clergy conducted services, and there were daily AA meetings. The sanctuary had a vaulted ceiling, polished wood pews, and a pine pulpit. In contrast, the chapel on death row was a small room encased in wire, about twelve by twenty-five feet. It had once been a shower. At the center of the room, three wooden benches were bolted to the floor, and there were three steel-mesh cages behind them. At the front, facing the benches and cages, was a sort of desk that served as a pulpit. Once again wearing a stab-proof vest, Susan Shannon stood behind it.

Armed guards watched from a gun rail as the room filled with tattooed, muscular men who talked and joked until Susan began speaking. When the inmates quieted, Susan instructed them to calm, center, and breathe.

She had developed a curriculum for teaching Buddhism in prison that included sections on its history, philosophy, and practice, everything from "What does Buddha mean?" and "How did the Buddha teach?" to the definitions of dharma and other Buddhist concepts. There were lessons about the Three Jewels and the Four Noble Truths, which she compared to "the disease, the diagnosis, the cure, and the medication," and she taught various forms of meditation, including one called the Equanimity Meditation to build compassion.

Susan asked the men to close their eyes, and she led them in the Equanimity Meditation. In a slow, measured, even voice, she said, "Start imagining someone in front of you who has neither helped nor harmed you, someone you neither like nor dislike—someone you have a neutral feeling for. Think to yourself, 'That person wants happiness, health, and good fortune, just like I do. They do not want suffering, hardship, famine, just like me.' Can you recognize a neutral feeling, a feeling of equanimity, neither aversion nor attraction? When you feel this equanimity to any degree, touch your hand to your heart, breathe in, and silently say to yourself, 'This feeling is equanimity, and it blesses me and those around me with peace and stillness.'"

She continued, "Now imagine someone in front of you whom you like. Think to yourself, 'That person wants happiness, health, and good fortune, just like me. They do not want suffering, hardship, famine, just like me.' Can you feel the same equanimity and neutrality toward them? Breathe in and out gently and evenly three times. Slowly scan your body from top of head to bottom of feet. If you find your breath shortening, note the location in your body where the breath encounters tightness. What memories are coming up for you right now? What emotions are coming up right now? When you feel any degree of equanimity toward the person you like, silently touch your heart and say, 'This feeling is equanimity, and it blesses me and those around me with peace and stillness.'"

The room was tranquil. The only sounds were Susan's voice and the inmates' rhythmic breathing.

She said, "Now imagine someone in front of you whom you really dislike. Breathe in and out gently and slowly three times. Slowly scan your body from top of head to bottom of feet. If you find your breath shortening, note the location in your body where the breath encounters tightness. What memories are coming up for you right now? What emotions are coming up right now? Think to yourself, 'That person wants happiness, health, and good fortune, just like me. They do not want suffering, hardship, famine, just like me.' When you feel any degree of equanimity toward that person you dislike, silently touch your heart and say, 'This feeling is equanimity, and it blesses me and those around me with peace and stillness.'"

Susan then instructed the men to imagine all three people together in front of them. "What does your equanimity feel like now? Do you feel more or less even? Remind yourself that yes, these three people, just like me, want the same positive qualities in life that I do. Breathe into that thought. Think to yourself, 'If all beings in the world could feel equanimity toward others, the world would be more at peace. It is my wish that through my feeling this even for a fleeting moment, I am offering just a little bit more peace and comfort to those around me. May I continue to have and hold equanimity in my life, so that I and those around me can feel and grow from the peace of this harmonious thought.'"

The meditation ended, and Susan told the men to take a deep breath and open their eyes.

She turned the class over to Jarvis. He'd spoken to her about what he wanted to talk about: how Buddhism had helped him "interrupt the patterns" that had led to all the trouble in his life and ultimately death row.

"If you always walk down the same road to the same street corner where there are drugs and guns, you'll always end up in the middle of drugs and guns," he told the group. "You can change things by walking down a different street." He continued, "It's different if you make a different plan, think things through. Revenge? Someone disses you, insults your sister, looks at you the wrong way. You react. That's a pattern. The next thing, you're fighting. Maybe you get a gun. You're back in the joint. Or dead. Or someone else is dead. But if you break the pattern and go another way, your life can go another way. Buddhism can teach you how. It prepares you in advance. You can be prepared before you go into the situation. If you're calmer, aware, conscious, thinking about cause and effect, you'll take that different street; or if you experience the same trigger that in the past would have put you instantly in that pattern—a word, something physical—now you can let it flow off your back. Like this: Some guy says something, you're in a place where you can fight or you can go 'He's not a bad person, maybe a little fucked up . . . let it go.' You take a breath."

Jarvis cited an example that made the men laugh: "The other day I was talking on the yard, and some con tells me I'm talking too loud. I'm ready to go off on him. In the old days, I would have. Before, there was no stop sign. But I've learned—I'm *learning*—to react differently. I've been able to slow things down.

"Later I was complaining to my Buddhist teacher about the guy who said I was talking too loud. She asked, 'What were you so excited about that you were talking so loud?'

"I'm laughing and thinking, 'Hell, maybe I *was* talking too loud.'"

When the men stopped laughing, Jarvis continued, "So this is how you change. If you become thoughtful—self-aware—you can interrupt something that would have triggered you. The more you can respond in a thoughtful way, the more you can"—he paused and looked around the room—"stay out of trouble."

Jarvis said that Buddhism had helped him in another way, too. "You look at people differently," he said. "A guard goes off on you. Instead of fighting, you think, 'That guy has had a hell of a day. That guy has had a hell of a life. He's struggling.' You look at him, and you shrug. You apologize to him. 'I'm sorry I bumped into you, man.' Now, that's not the reaction he expects. That trips him up."

As the class came to a close, Susan led the men in a final meditation, and then guards came, chained the inmates, and led them away.

Susan led the classes most weeks, and though some men dropped out, most stayed. Jarvis was allowed to attend only some, but he was in several classes with a murderer who each week came to the chapel with a stack of Buddhist books and readings. Talking about dharma as if he were a scholar and meanwhile misusing Tibetan words and mantras and mischaracterizing Buddhist principles, the man dominated the classes. Jarvis found him pompous and annoying.

One evening, the man made Jarvis especially angry. Back in his cell after class, he thought about why he'd bothered him so much.

He envisioned the man, and then in his mind he looked directly into his eyes. When he did, he saw a man on death row like himself. The man was confused and scared. No wonder he clutched those books so tightly.

Jarvis smiled with the recognition that the inmate was a truer Buddhist than he was, because the man was in the middle of his suffering, whereas Jarvis had stepped away from his and was judging the man as if he knew better. Jarvis realized that he had nothing to teach the man; the man was teaching *him*.

Alan Senauke once told Jarvis a story about Nan-in, a Japanese Zen master who lived a hundred years ago. A university professor came to the teacher to ask about Zen. "Nan-in served tea. He poured his visitor's cup full, and then kept on pouring. The professor watched it overflow and spill onto the table until he no longer could restrain himself. 'It is overfull,' he said. 'No more will go in!'

"Like this cup," Nan-in said, "you are full of your own opinions and speculations. How can I show you Zen unless you first empty your cup?"

How could Jarvis learn if he'd become so full of his own ideas about what a Buddhist was and should be? Alan had given him the book *Zen Mind, Beginner's Mind*, in which another Sōtō monk, Shunryū Suzuki, had written, "If your mind is empty, it is always ready for anything, it is open to everything. In the beginner's mind there are many possibilities, but in the expert's mind there are few." Jarvis had come upon another Buddha he had to kill.

*　　*　　*

On a cold fall morning, Susan Shannon arrived at Jarvis's cell and watched him drag himself out of bed to come to the door. He looked weary and gaunt, and she asked what was wrong. Jarvis told her about a man who'd been moved into the cell next to his; Jarvis knew him as Thomas.*

"Listen," he said. Susan listened, and she heard sharp, wheezing, guttural coughing.

Jarvis said that the coughing never stopped, and Thomas kept him awake with his rasping and choking. He'd asked Thomas what was going on, and his neighbor said he had stage four throat cancer.

"Why aren't you in the hospital if you're so sick?" Jarvis had asked.

"I've been there. There's nothing they can do for me."

Later Jarvis whispered to a guard, "So you're just going to keep him here to die?" The guard shrugged. "I wish there was something I could do, but it's not my decision."

Jarvis talked to Thomas sometimes, asked how he was doing, but the man could barely respond. Sometimes it sounded as if he were choking to death.

"I know he's in pain, dying. But the noise doesn't stop," Jarvis said. "It's like nails are being pounded into my head. It's hard to fall asleep, and then an hour or two later I wake up because he's hacking. I can't write; I can't meditate."

Susan said, "You're practicing in a place where you're living

*"Thomas" is a pseudonym.

among the suffering of lives lost, dreams lost, families and futures lost; the suffering of remorse and regret, old age and dying, the suffering of guards, and the suffering of pain and causing pain. You don't want to deny it—to close off from it—but you have to protect yourself." She told Jarvis she'd learned to call on Red Tara whenever she came into the prison and felt the weight of the suffering inside its walls. In the same way that Tara helped her continue to give of herself but protect herself, she could help Jarvis remain compassionate while guarding himself. "You want to feel others' suffering," she said, "but not drown in it. Then you're no good to anyone."

Then she explained how she protected herself. Every time she walked through the San Quentin gates, she imagined herself surrounded by a "pearlescent membrane" as she recited the Red Tara prayer. She envisioned the membrane as a one-way mirror. It allowed her to fulfill her Buddhist commitment "to extend to all beings" and at the same time to protect herself from being consumed. She suggested that Jarvis try it with his neighbor, to find his own one-way mirror, so he could remain open to Thomas's suffering and also protect himself so he could sleep and focus.

Jarvis tried, but Thomas's health deteriorated, and his cough got even worse. Jarvis thought he should have gotten used to it by now, but he simply couldn't. As his exhaustion increased, so did his anger.

One night, Jarvis managed to fall asleep, only to wake up suddenly a few hours later. It took him a while to realize that Thomas's coughing hadn't woken him. Its absence had.

Thomas must have died.

Jarvis sat up and tried to absorb the fact that his neighbor was dead.

It might have been a minute, but it felt like forever, before Jarvis heard a sharp gasp. He held his breath and listened. Another gasp and then the hacking cough, as loud as ever. Louder. Jarvis felt a rush of relief.

All he'd wanted was for the noise to end, but now he rejoiced in its return.

After that, whatever Jarvis did, whether meditating, writing, *anything*, he did it with Thomas's belabored breath as background noise. He celebrated it. It was the sound of life.

PART FOUR

THE FOURTH NOBLE TRUTH

THE PATH

My religion is very simple. My religion is kindness.

—Dalai Lama

18

HOPE

Jarvis knew that Pamela had been sick. When, in the fall of 2014, he learned that she had amyloidosis, an infection of the blood, he called a friend and asked him to research the disease. He wanted to know how long Pamela had to live.

As her illness progressed, Pamela continued her biweekly visits, even when a CO had to drive her from the entrance to East Block in a golf cart. But though she'd been ill, her death was sudden and shocking. One day, her heart just stopped. Pamela's friends remembered her inimitable, irreverent spirit. In part, her obituary read, "She was born into privilege, but hardly ever invoked it, except to park wherever she pleased, no matter the signage or curb color, and to drive without regard for speed limits and painted lines." One of her friends said that it would be fitting if Pamela's ashes were spread at San Quentin and Bergdorf Goodman (they were).

Pema and Marie brought Jarvis the news. They sat together for a while, comforting each other, and then Marie left so Pema and Jarvis could be alone. They sat for two hours, reminisced about Pamela, and cried.

Jarvis reflected on her hundreds of visits, her advocacy, her efforts to publicize his case, and her tenacity. He recalled the stories she had entertained him with, and the way her family had become his family. He described years of laughter and tears and the thousand Diet Cokes she drank during their visits. They spoke about the time she ignored the lawyers and Melody and called Judge Savitt and asked her out to lunch.

Pema asked him if he'd like to say something at the Sukhavati ceremony (a Buddhist funeral) she would be conducting later that week. Jarvis wrote about her on a napkin: "Every two weeks for 17 years she came to see me on Tuesday. . . . I will forever hear her laugh. . . . She never gave me the slightest chance to doubt that she loved me & that I was part of her family. There will never be anyone like her."

That day, the guards made a point of staying back from the cage, giving them privacy, and allowing them more time than scheduled. When Jarvis was finally led away, Pema noticed that the guard applied handcuffs to his wrists with unusual delicacy.

Jarvis remained in his cell for days and thought about Pamela being gone—forever. Marie was a great champion, but Pamela had been dedicated for almost two decades.

Now that he had phone privileges, Jarvis would call Pema whenever the demons came—whenever he was especially sad, angry, depressed, or desperate. Her quiet voice soothed him. That was all it took sometimes—hearing her.

Now he needed to talk with her about Pamela, but Pema was traveling, and he couldn't reach her. Feeling he'd lost his greatest ally in Pamela, fearing abandonment, he began to panic, but then he did what Pema would have wanted him to do. He sat on the ground, took a deep breath, and began to meditate. He envisioned Pema's smile and eyes; they radiated loving acceptance. In that state, he realized he'd come up with his own mantra: "What would Pema say?" He realized that her voice had joined Chagdud Tulku's inside him. What would Pema say then? She'd tell him to face the fears and experience the grief. She'd tell him to sit. He did and allowed himself to cry hard until he felt Pamela's presence soothing him.

Later, when he finally reached Pema, he told her he'd discovered that her voice was inside his head. She said, "That's not my voice, Jarvis. It's *your* voice. It's always been there. Now you can hear it."

Pamela's husband, Marty, came to visit that week, and they sat together quietly, talking about Pamela. Jarvis told Marty that he'd been unable to leave his cell. Marty nodded, said he understood, and then said that he knew that Pamela would have wanted him to engage in life—to go out on the yard and feel the sun. The next day he did. The fog felt cool and soothing. Leaning on the fence, he thought about the many times he'd heard Buddhists talking about reincarnation, which had never made sense to him. When they talked about reincarnation, he thought about recycling cans and bottles, his father's business. But by then he'd realized he didn't have to believe in a literal life after death to understand that the concept is true in at least one way. It was true of Chagdud Tulku and of his mother. Like them, Pamela was alive inside him and in the hearts of everyone who loved her. He corrected himself: "Who *love* her."

Not long after Pamela's death, Joe Baxter was informed by the California Supreme Court that the court had approved his request for a review of the 2011 evidentiary hearing. In a filing, Joe had argued that the court had been capricious, inconsistent, and biased in its decisions about which evidence and witnesses were allowed and which weren't. He also raised the arbitrariness in the application of the death penalty. Jarvis had been convicted of conspiracy and fashioning the knife used in the murder and had been sentenced to death, but his codefendants, including the man who actually stabbed the guard, had received lighter sentences: life in prison without the possibility of parole.

Once again, the lawyers were optimistic. The court wouldn't have agreed to review the hearing if it hadn't found merit in Baxter's arguments. Rick Targow identified another reason for hope: the earlier court had been mostly made up of judges appointed by tough-on-crime Republican governors, but the current governor, Jerry Brown, had appointed far more progressive judges; it was the first liberal California Supreme Court in two decades.

The hearing was to take place at the state courthouse in Sacramento. After Baxter presented his oral arguments, the court would have ninety days to respond. Jarvis girded for another battle with his formidable enemy, hope.

From the outside, Jarvis seemed okay for the first couple of weeks, but under the stoic facade he was in agony, trying to hold up a dam on the other side of which was terror. He knew he could hold it up for only so long before it would burst.

Pema heard fragility in his voice. He'd always been resilient, but how much disappointment could a person take? Jarvis was as devoted a practitioner as anyone she'd ever known, but she worried about him. Could the Buddha himself maintain his equilibrium while anticipating a ruling with such high stakes?

In the past, Jarvis's friends had remarked that his spirit seemed inexhaustible, but three weeks in, it was evident that the pressure was taking a toll—the dam was breached. Jarvis was exhausted from erratic sleep as his anxiety about the hearing mounted.

By then he understood how poisonous hope could be, but he couldn't help hope, playing out the scenarios he wished for: justice, freedom. He told Susan that he'd watched men killed by hope. "Cons are told time and time again that they're getting out. Then they're disappointed. The cycle only stops when they kill themselves."

Susan responded, "I get it. I understand how hope can be poison. But would you ever want to have no hope?"

It was another Buddhist mindfuck. Yes, who would want to live without hope?

Hope? No hope? His confusion intensified. He thought, *Again?*

More riddles? Don't you have anything more for me? I'm so tired of this. "I can't do it," he said. "Look at me. I've been meditating for thirty fucking years—more—and I'm back where I started."

Lisa Leghorn once told him that the repetition of teachings is essential and inherent in Tibetan meditation, and that with repetition "the teachings of Buddhism blend with our minds and hearts until we become one with them." She said, "Ideas change first, and then our experience of reality changes." And then we start again. It's like *Groundhog Day*. It may seem like you've made no progress and are starting over, but you aren't. Every repetition is different; the lessons are different because you are.

When Jarvis told Pema that he was unable to detach from the hope that the hearing would go his way, she reminded him, "Not being attached doesn't mean not feeling. The point is not to deny yourself your feelings, not to shut yourself down and pretend you aren't human." She counseled, "Sit with the feeling of hope. Yes, again. Again. Allow it in, don't block it, don't pretend it's not happening." She said to keep busy doing what he loved and to focus on others—to try to find ways to help people—because that's the surest way out of self-obsession.

A week went by. Another. His anxiety increased. Forget about sleep. His mind spun out by day, but night was worse. On one of those nights he realized that he was trapped in the same psychic thicket that had snared him during the 2011 hearing: he feared both remaining in prison and getting out of it.

In the morning he called Pema and said something he'd only say to her because she was the only one who would fully understand. "I'm afraid to say it," he said. "If I say it, it'll sound like I don't want to get out of here. I do. So bad. And even more important, I want people to know I'm innocent. So I keep thinking about losing and having to face that. But when I think about winning and walking out of San Quentin—that scares the hell out of me, too."

"The real question," Pema said, "is if it's possible to feel both things at the same time. Buddhism teaches us that we can. Ambivalence is truer than certainty. Allow yourself to feel both. Don't fight it. If you do, you're fighting yourself."

Jarvis's turmoil continued unabated, but there was a respite when he next heard from Thomas. Jarvis had been worried for several months since guards took his neighbor to the hospital. He learned he was having intensive chemotherapy but received no more news until one day when he heard Thomas's voice calling him.

"Hey, man. Left Hand? You there?"

Jarvis's heart leapt. "Hey, brother!" he called out. "How the hell are you? Been missing you down here."

Jarvis was elated to hear the news: his neighbor's cancer had gone into remission. Given the earlier prognosis, it was miraculous. Thomas had gotten a reprieve. Jarvis thought, *This whole Buddhist trip is that death will come—it always does. But in the meantime, there's life. And damn that's a good thing.*

The weeks of waiting rolled forward. Marie visited when she could. He didn't tell her about his fear of getting out. Instead, sitting opposite each other with their hands clasped, they discussed their plans for when he would be freed.

For half the time they'd known each other, Jarvis had been in the AC, so when they first met, there was a glass partition between them. Since he'd been moved to East Block, they met in a barred cage with see-through plastic walls. There was no privacy. They'd never been alone. What would it be like to truly be alone with her? He didn't even know if he could sleep in an actual bed anymore.

Their relationship had been tested by unnatural and surreal circumstances. Could it survive normal ones? They'd never been physically intimate. Death row prisoners don't have conjugal visits.

Jarvis's meals had been brought to him since he was nineteen years old. He didn't know how to shop. Pamela had gotten him a hot plate, but he couldn't remember how to use a stove.

Jarvis recalled when he was first moved to East Block, where he initially felt overwhelmed and wanted to go back to the AC. Having become accustomed to the complete enclosure of his cell in solitary, he felt exposed and vulnerable in a cell that opened onto the tier. The sense of exposure was even more pronounced on the comparatively enormous East Block yard. His first time out, he could take only a dozen steps before he froze in fear. Outside prison, he'd be faced with an infinite number of steps.

He'd read stories of inmates released after decades who reoffended so they could go back to a life they knew and others who committed suicide after they got out. Would he fare better than they had?

Jarvis had his friends. He believed he could rely on them. But could he? Would they remain his friends?

He worried about work. How would he earn a living? Was he qualified to do anything? After his two books, could he make money as a writer? He had a lot to say about the prison system, solitary confinement, the impact of prison and the interminable appeals process on inmates and their families, and the transformative power of Buddhism. But could he actually be a writer on the outside? He thought more about working with kids—the boxing gym. Maybe he could do that.

Then he felt a shiver when he thought about sitting with Marie in a restaurant or café. He'd have to sit with his back to the wall, or he'd be so anxious he'd run out. Paranoia was the default state in prison. He'd been looking over his shoulder since he was a child. He worried that he'd become so institutionalized that he actually needed the presence of bars and guards to feel secure. Outside there'd be no one watching over him, ready to stop an attack. That thought appalled him. Did he feel safer in San Quentin than he would in the outside world? How fucked up was that?

Marie visited once and sometimes twice a week. Jarvis saw in the paleness of her skin and the dark circles under her eyes that the anticipation was wearing on her, too. She always said she was fine, but he saw the truth. She wasn't sleeping, either, and maybe not eating. They were on the same roller coaster, hoping for the best, trying not to think of the worst, and meanwhile she planned what she'd cook for him his first night home. She bought new sheets and pillowcases and bought him slippers and a bathrobe.

Marie pictured where they'd live, in her home in the Sunset District of San Francisco, near Golden Gate Park, from which they could walk to the beach. Or should they rent a cabin in the country somewhere, where he could acclimate slowly to life outside?

Sometimes she cried, but not the tears she'd shed for years when she'd left San Quentin alone, without her husband. Now she cried with the joy of imagining them together at last. She would take him to the places she loved: Big Sur, Yosemite, and the Painted Desert. She pictured them walking on the beach at night.

Jarvis wasn't allowed to attend the hearing, but on the morning of the oral argument on November 13, 2015, a dozen of his friends caravanned to Sacramento to listen to Joe present the arguments. Alan drove with Marty. As he'd done at the evidentiary hearing, Alan took notes and reported about the day on his blog.

Speaking in his usual easy drawl, Joe presented an overview of Jarvis's case and outlined the arguments presented in the filing. He asked the court to "right the terrible injustice that has been done to Jarvis Jay Masters." Joe addressed some of the referees' conclusions and referred the judges to the full filing. He spoke for the allotted twenty minutes.

On the drive home, Marty and Alan dissected the presentation. They felt optimistic that the justices would find the initial trial a travesty and Jarvis's innocence irrefutable. First, though, there would be another period of waiting. The court had ninety days to decide.

After all his years of practice, Jarvis believed a Buddhist should be better at weathering uncertainty, but he confided to Alan, "This is the hardest time I've ever done."

"Harder than twenty-one years in the hole?"

Jarvis nodded. "Hopelessness was normal in the hole. It was easier to be hopeless."

A week more. Two. He tried to hang on to the middle—not to freak out. He and Marie talked more about their life together after he got out. Jarvis began packing his possessions—literally packing them in boxes. He thought about to whom in the prison he'd bequeath his CDs. One of his friends didn't have a decent TV, so he'd give him his. He'd give away the posters on the wall, the teakettle, the extra blankets Pamela had sent, and his library.

The three months clicked by, one excruciating day at a time. As the ninetieth day approached, Rick told him that the court released its decisions on Mondays and Thursdays. Thursday came and there was no decision, so Jarvis had to make it through one of the longest weekends of his life.

Marie came, and they were both so nervous that they barely said a word throughout the hour-and-a-half visit. He and Pema spoke frequently. Speaking to her always helped, and he tried to follow her advice. He fought to meditate. He spent Friday night awake and, feeling the hardness of his mattress and listening to an argument on the tier, did meditate—though prone—as well as he could. He felt panic attacks coming and averted them by slow, deep breathing.

He made it to Saturday morning, when he spoke to friends on the phone. That afternoon, he watched TV but couldn't concentrate. Reading was impossible. Another sleepless night, and then Marie visited again on Sunday. That night he must have drifted off, because he awoke an hour later reeling from a nightmare. He was wearing a light-colored short-sleeved shirt and white pants, carrying a small duffel bag with his few possessions. The sky was shining blue. He was flanked by guards for the last time. They held his upper arms as they led him down one and then another corridor. He looked anxiously ahead, anticipating the sight of his friends who'd be waiting for him. They'd hug, cry, and leave together. He'd look over his shoulder—it would be his final image of San Quentin. Just as they reached the gate, the officers stopped short and pushed him forward. It was all wrong. He realized they'd tricked him and pushed him into the execution chamber. He turned to flee, but they'd sealed the door.

Jarvis sat up on his bunk. It was 4:00 a.m., Monday, February 26, 2016, still dark outside, but a dull orange-gray light bathed the cellblock. Jarvis sat and meditated, took in the deepest breaths he could, and let the air carry the fear out in a slow, clear stream.

Scott Kauffman, the lawyer with CAP, had an appointment to see him and would report the outcome. Scott waited in the parking lot for the decision to be announced. An email arrived, and Scott went inside.

Waiting in a cage, Jarvis looked at Scott with painful hope, which evaporated instantly. Scott confirmed what Jarvis had read in his face: the court had affirmed the judgment in its entirety. The decision was unanimous. All of Jarvis's claims had been rejected.

19

LETTING GO

Scott departed, and Jarvis was led to his cell. When he was locked inside and the guard left, he felt faint and steadied himself by leaning on the wall. He sat and held his throat. He felt as if he were drowning. He struggled to keep from passing out.

Five years earlier, he'd been disappointed by the result of the evidentiary hearing, but this defeat felt worse. As far as he could recall, he wasn't this devastated even when Judge Savitt sentenced him to death. Why? Maybe it was just that he'd been so young then and couldn't comprehend the enormity of the punishment. Or maybe he was just older and wearier.

The next day Jarvis spoke to Alan, who encouraged him: "This is a setback but by no means the last word." Jarvis spoke to Rick, who said he shouldn't lose heart; this decision just cleared the way for the next stage of the appeal, the habeas corpus hearing. When Jarvis finally spoke to Joe Baxter, Joe promised they'd win the next round and said, "Just hold tight." Jarvis hung up on him.

Jarvis called Pema, and they cried together. "I wish I could be sitting with you, Jarvis. There's no way to make these bad feelings go away now," she said sadly. "You want them to, but you have to go through them. I wish you didn't. But even as you do, remember earlier times you were in distress—how every time you came out the other side. You are a warrior."

Jarvis said nothing, but she knew what he was thinking. She said, "I know you don't feel like a warrior, but you are, and sometimes a warrior's task is to sit with defeat." When the automated voice on the phone warned that the call would end in fifteen seconds, Pema said, "I'm here, Jarvis. I love you."

He answered weakly. "I love you, Mama."

Then Marie visited. She cried, too. Sitting with her, watching her, holding her hand, and witnessing her anguish broke Jarvis's heart. As illogical as it was, he felt as if he'd let her down, and he apologized. They'd been together fifteen years, married for half that time. She had been certain—*certain*—that he'd win this round. She believed that the case was clear-cut and Jarvis would either be freed or, at the least, granted a new trial. The blanket dismissal felt like a brutal slap across her face.

Jarvis watched that face—drained, frail, weary—and for the first time saw the profound depth of her sadness. This defeat might be too hard for her to bear—what if she gave up? Pamela had been his greatest and most consistent champion for decades, but she was gone. Pema truly was like a mother. Melody, Alan, Susan, and other friends were devoted to him, but there'd never been anyone like Marie in his life. He'd never felt as protected and well cared for—and as well loved. But how long would she wait? How long *should* she wait? Was it fair to her? The loss in court devastated him. He didn't know if he could endure losing her, too. Then he thought, *I'm in prison. She doesn't have to be. You don't want that for the person you love.*

Jarvis spoke to other friends on the phone, and some visited. When they expressed their sorrow, he said, "It's going to be okay." He was reassuring *them!* Inmates on the tier encouraged him. "You were fucked over," one said. A message from Freddie Taylor was delivered by a con on Jarvis's tier. "I heard what happened, brother," Freddie said. "Don't give up." Jarvis appreciated the support but felt disconnected from everyone. He felt as if he were encased in glass and his friends—everyone—were on the outside. Only Pema was able to penetrate it when he called her each day. Other than her, Jarvis felt alone, and he sunk further into a kind of depression he'd never known before. He told Pema, using the word *depression*, one he'd avoided in the past. He admitted that he didn't know if he could survive. He admitted that he didn't know if he wanted to.

Jarvis refused yard time and didn't eat. He tried to meditate, but it was a perfunctory attempt. He sat and closed his eyes, but he lacked the energy to focus on his breath. Actually, there was barely enough breath on which to focus.

*　　*　　*

Across the bay in San Francisco, Marie was miserable, too. Like Jarvis, she could hardly get out of bed, and she took a leave from her job. Jarvis called a few times. They rehashed the court's ruling, trying to fathom why he'd lost. Sometimes they held the phone to their ears but didn't speak because there was nothing to say. They felt broken both individually and as a couple. Jarvis tried not to acknowledge what he knew to be true: that the state had taken his liberty, and it would take his marriage. When she visited, he said, "I'll understand if you have to move on." She answered with tears.

After the visit, Jarvis called Pema. Her voice soothed him. As always when he suffered and stopped meditating, she gently encouraged him to sit. "I can't," Jarvis insisted. "I'm just here trying to survive."

"That," Pema said, "is the reason to meditate."

"But, Mama," Jarvis pleaded. "I've done it all these years, and look where I am. Everyone's saying I'm this Buddhist living here on death row, like I'm above all the moods, no disappointment, riding the wave, doing the trip, saying the words, transcending this place, but it isn't real. I am pretending. I felt if I pretended maybe it would become true—free your mind and all that—but it hasn't. I didn't want to disappoint Rinpoche. I don't want to disappoint you."

"You could never disappoint me," she said. "I've been in this business a long time, and I haven't ever met anyone who tries harder than you. I'm in awe of the way you've kept your spirit alive. I don't know how you've done it. It says everything about who you are—your nature, your heart."

He said, "Yeah, well, I don't know if I can do it anymore." For the first time, Jarvis was thinking about—talking about—stopping. That is, stopping pretending he was a Buddhist. The significance of the moment was not lost on Pema, but she brought him back to familiar ground, terrain they had walked together many times. "You're doing what you need to do; you're feeling the pain. It's just hard. There's no way around that."

Jarvis didn't call Marie for a week. He was inside his head and couldn't break out. Prisoners can make calls but not receive them, so she waited. She understood his agony, but being cut off was hard for her. She imagined him in his cell, depressed, and wished they could have shared their sadness.

Meanwhile, Jarvis reminisced about her. He recalled her being with him in the cage, sitting across from him, their hands locked, and her tenderness. He thought again about how much she'd done for him and how it wasn't fair to her that she was in a relationship that was limited to phone calls, letters, and visits in a cage. His anger welled up—he hated San Quentin. He thought, *They're keeping my wife in prison, on death row, not just me. I have to do time, but she doesn't. You don't want that for your best friend.*

Jarvis was in tears when he finally called. Her voice was weak. "What have you been thinking?" she asked.

"That I love you," he said. "And that's why we should get a divorce."

At first she didn't respond. Then she asked why.

"You've been waiting for me to get out of here. It looks like it won't be for a while. You got to go on with your life. I gotta go on with mine."

She cried and said, "Jarvis, I don't know."

"*I* know," he said. Then he hung up.

Jarvis hid in his cell. He talked to Pema. He felt drained and—yes, that word—hopeless. When he next called Marie he said, "We should do it."

"Do it?"

"Put the divorce through." She cried but didn't disagree. He asked her if she'd take care of the paperwork and said he'd sign when she did.

Jarvis trembled when he hung up. It was the right thing to do, but where did it leave him? An empty feeling rose inside him, one familiar from earlier in his life that he had all but forgotten. The terror—it was the only word—flooded him, and he almost started to hyperventilate. He knew he had Pema and his other friends, but with Marie he had a legal spouse who could check on him when others couldn't because the prison was locked down. With Marie he had a picture of the future when he got out. Through her he'd been intimately and continuously connected with the world outside San Quentin in a way that no other bond could provide. And now that connection was gone. As he'd been so many times in the past, he was alone, and he was petrified. He sat down to meditate. He remembered *tonglen* and decided to try it. As he'd learned to do, when he breathed in he imagined sucking in his sadness. He felt it like the poison Pema had described. He sucked it all the way down into the depths of his lungs and then realized that he wasn't only drawing in his sadness but all people's sadness. What came next in *tonglen*? He breathed out what he needed and all people needed: the warmth and protection of Red Tara, a connection with others, gentleness, and love. He repeated the process—again, again—and eventually realized he was going to be okay.

He and Pema spoke that afternoon. He told her about the experience meditating. He said he'd also been thinking about Marie and realized he was breathing out what she needed to heal, too. And he'd had a revelation: "When I said we should divorce, I thought I was freeing her, but I was freeing myself, too. This hoping and planning wasn't just a burden on her but on me. I was having to hold her up, act like I was sure I'd get out, making those plans. I wanted them to be true, but also I didn't want to hurt or disappoint her. That was a burden. I'm not in a place where I can hold anyone else up." He continued, "The problem isn't love. I love her, and I know she loves me. But what if I choose not to focus on getting out but on where my life is? Would I be abandoning our dream and my commitment to her? If we get a divorce, I won't have to carry her disappointment. I don't want to carry anyone now. I can't."

He felt he couldn't because he had to focus on surviving. He'd figured out how. The *tonglen* practice had guided him. He had to take in his own and the world's poison and breathe out what could help him and everyone else. What could help them? He would have to leave his cell and engage again.

Pema responded, "You've told me about how many men have lost their minds since you've been here. You've told me about men in the AC howling and smashing their heads against the walls, men cowering in the corner of their cell every day and night and living in paranoia and rage. You've told me about all the guys who are addicted and all the suicides. You could have gone those ways but didn't. You survived, which is miraculous on its own, but it's not only that you survived, Jarvis. You still have your mind, your wisdom, and your beautiful spirit. You still have your laughter. And here's the main thing: it's understandable that you want to walk in open space but remember that you have the ability to go there now."

Pema raised a central Buddhist concept, *samsara*, the cycle of birth and death in which humans are trapped because of their desires, fears, and ignorance, until they reach Nirvana, when they no longer have those desires and fears and have attained the wisdom that brings enlightenment.

"In Buddhism, just as Christianity, there is a notion of hell, but in Buddhism it's not a literal place—no fire and devil—but a state of mind where there's unceasing suffering. But in that hell there's always a Buddha in the middle of the suffering as he works to alleviate it. He's not put off by hell and is willing to help and able to help. I feel like you're like that, Jarvis. You're right in the middle of the hell of San Quentin; and you're able to help the people here. You help people in hell. Do you know who else does that? The Buddha."

That night Jarvis's meditation took him to his childhood again. He was four years old, maybe younger. He was still living with his mother and was playing in the bedroom one day when he went into a closet, looked up, and saw the outline of a panel in the ceiling. He climbed on top of the boxes and clothes, pushed the panel open, and entered the crawl space. He reveled in the quiet and feeling of safety.

After that, when he sensed a dangerous shift in the adults' moods, someone getting high, sharp voices that were the prelude to a fight, or the sounds of men in bed with his mother, he would go into the closet and climb up, seeking refuge in the secret small, dark space.

In his meditation, he was again in the crawl space, which morphed into his cell. He had a startling thought: He'd spent his life seeking out spaces to hide in, where he'd be safe, making himself as small as he could, and those crawl spaces were prisons, jails, and solitary confinement. The thought chilled him.

He became aware that he was meditating. The pause. He realized where he was and where he'd gone, and he breathed deeply. When he opened his eyes, he saw something—another of those profound feelings that seemed to come out of the blue since he'd embarked on the Buddhist path. He closed his eyes again and breathed with the intention of staying focused and present, but he returned to the story he'd been in. He was back in time a couple of months before, when he'd been awaiting the court's decision. He watched himself packing his possessions, giving some away, and preparing to give away the rest. When the court denied his claims, he looked around his bare cell, furious with himself for the delusional hope that had moved him to empty it. But now he grasped the unthinking wisdom behind his actions. He'd thought he was emptying his cell because he'd be leaving San Quentin, but really he'd been emptying it because he was staying.

Jarvis often recalled Chagdud Tulku telling him that we never know who our most important teachers will be, and the Dalai Lama had once said that our *enemies* are our most important teachers. By that logic, his most recent teacher was the California Supreme Court. When it denied his appeal, saying in essence, "We're not going to let you out—not yet," he realized he had to free *himself*.

ENLIGHTENMENT

Jarvis wrote Pema, "I meditated this morning. For three hours. I got there again. It's like there's this sadness, this loss, but lightness. It's like I'm throwing off these rocks I've been carrying. The rocks are the ideas about what I think I need in my life to be happy."

He expanded on that notion when they talked on the phone. "My fantasy has been that getting out will bring me happiness," he said. "It's always something—I think we all do it. We think if we get what we want we'll be happy. We fantasize that a relationship will bring us happiness. We think we'll find fulfillment, an end to our suffering, and we can stop running and we'll sleep soundly all night. But I see the truth in letters people write me. They're chasing that illusion of happiness. They have the two-car garage, the beachfront home, their perfect children and cute dog, and they still feel depression. If you have everything and still are depressed, now, that's a bigger problem than what I have. You have all that, and you're feeling shitty? That's not freedom. I'm freer than that."

Jarvis acknowledged that there were many privileges of freedom from prison that he craved: visiting a forest or seaside, walking wherever he wanted to with no chains or cuffs and no guard at his elbow, eating a fresh peach (he hadn't had one since he was a child).

He said he'd like to turn a doorknob.

Pema was surprised. "Turn a doorknob?"

"I haven't opened or closed a door for more than thirty-five years. I would like to open my own doors and be free in that way." Then he said, "I know what you'll say: I have the ability to open my own doors now. I get that, but I'd still like to open an actual door by myself. But we all have lists of what we think we need in order to be happy. The thing is, when you get something on the list, you want something else. It never ends."

Jarvis told Pema a story about his childhood. In the front room of his grandmother's house in Harbor City there had always been a bowl of apples and oranges. He'd run by and grab one. When he lived with one of the foster families, there was a bowl of fruit on the dining table, too. He grabbed an apple and bit into it, and he was shocked: it was plastic. A fake. He thought that plastic fruit must be what wealthy people have. Poor people couldn't buy plastic fruit with food stamps. "But then I thought, *It's better to have an apple you can bite into.*"

Jarvis concluded, "Comparing yourself to others, you never win. People always have described me as this stereotype: poverty, no food, no father, prostitute mother, beaten. They feel sorry for me. They shouldn't feel sorry for me.

"It doesn't matter where you are if you're suffering. Either way, you have the same job to do. You know how I never understood karma? Now, *that's* karma: wherever you are, you have to face yourself."

Jarvis realized that he'd emerged from survival mode, where he'd been since the devastating decision. He'd survived. He renewed his familiar and comforting routine. He began every morning with prostrations, and then he meditated. Then he did yoga, studied, and wrote. He went out on the yard again, talked with friends, and sought out cons who might need his help, whether they were missing home, afraid, angry, or simply depressed. And he returned to Susan's Buddhism class, studying and teaching those who attended a faith that he had tailor-made for prison.

Jarvis saw his friends regularly and appreciated them more than ever. The celebrated writer Rebecca Solnit often went rowing on the San Francisco Bay, and her route took her past San Quentin. Each time she paddled her kayak by the prison, she thought of Jarvis, whom she'd read about and once saw when she attended his 2007 hearing with a group of his Buddhist supporters. For her column in *Harper's Magazine*, Rebecca decided to write about the contrast between her "maximum freedom" gliding on the bay and Jarvis's "maximum unfreedom." She knew Melody, who told her how to get in touch with him. She and Jarvis began talking on the phone, and she visited him.

Once, Jarvis happened to call when Rebecca was hiking in New Mexico. Holding the phone to her ear, she walked him up Mt. Atalaya and described what she saw: the vistas and "glittering mica-strewn soil." In January 2017, he called when Rebecca was at San Francisco International Airport participating in a protest against an executive order by President Trump that blocked immigrants from Muslim countries from entering the United States. Rebecca asked Jarvis if he'd like to join the march, and she switched on the speaker-phone. He reveled in taking part. As someone whose political voice had been silenced for more than thirty-five years—he was one of America's six million felons who can't vote—he was participating in US democracy for the first time in his life.

Once Jarvis called Marty and Pamela's daughter, Samantha, when she was at the top of the Seattle Space Needle, and she described the breathtaking view. Another friend, Corny Koehl, was at a massive outdoor concert at the Five Point Amphitheater in Irvine, California, when Jarvis called. Corny held her phone up and Jarvis joined the throngs rocking out to ZZ Top, Lynyrd Skynyrd, and Cheap Trick.

Lee Lesser, a teacher and therapist who'd written him after reading *Finding Freedom,* was another close friend. Jarvis called Lee one Sunday afternoon when the cellblock was especially noisy because of the many inmates' TVs tuned to a Warriors game. Since most of those on the tier were occupied with the game, Jarvis was able to keep the phone longer than usual.

"We're all here," Lee said when she answered. "The whole family and a bunch of friends are here for a Passover seder, and we're just sitting down to dinner."

Jarvis apologized for interrupting, but Lee stopped him. "No, no, that's not what I was saying. I was just telling you what's going on." She said, "You're staying for dinner unless you have other plans!"

Lee placed a speakerphone at the center of the table and went around and introduced Jarvis to her guests. He listened to the prayers and songs and shared in the discussion and jokes. When the guests heard a loud roar over the speakerphone, one asked if prisoners were rioting. Jarvis said there must have been a basket.

Calls from death row are interrupted by a recorded voice that reminds the parties that the phone is monitored, and they're disconnected after fifteen minutes. Each time the phone cut off, Jarvis called back. He spent forty-five minutes participating in the seder by phone. When a guard came to retrieve it, Jarvis thanked Lee and her family.

That night he basked in the fellowship he'd felt during the seder. Then he tuned in to the noises on the tier, which were quieter after the game. His mind went to the men with whom he lived. When he was first put on death row, there were a few dozen; now there were more than seven hundred. Knowing that few if any would ever have a phone call like the one he'd just had, his heart broke for them, and he recalled again how lucky he was.

Several weeks later, Pema visited on the anniversary of Pamela's death so they could mark the occasion together. Before going into the cage that morning, she bought Jarvis snacks from the vending machine, choosing the only remotely healthy option, a fruit cocktail cup; Mom wants her son to eat healthier. She bought herself a bottle of water and a candy bar, because she sometimes needed an energy boost in the middle of a long visit. They embraced for a long time and then sat together holding hands.

Pema remarked on Jarvis's haircut: "It's like a monk!"

"It wasn't a religious decision," he said, laughing. "I messed up. My hand slipped when I was using a buzzer, and it carved a path down the middle. I had to live with that or shave the rest."

They reminisced about their departed friend; then they caught each other up on the doings of their families.

Harline had visited Jarvis the week before. "We were talking about our relatives," Jarvis told her. "'He died.' 'She passed away.' 'He's in the pen somewhere.' 'He's nuttier than a fruitcake.' 'He's an SOB.' 'She popped out another one—seven kids; the baby looks just like his mother, poor thing.'

"We were laughing our asses off—people were all staring. Then he started talking about his recycling business, and I could see him staring at the big plastic garbage cans with empty soda cans spilling out. I could tell he was thinking, 'Now, that's a gold mine,' and then he said it: 'Son, do you know what they do with all those Coke cans? That would be a hell of a business. Who would I talk to, son?'"

When guards walked a prisoner past the cage, Pema remarked on the man's extravagantly tattooed face and head, which prompted her to tell Jarvis about her recent visit to Homeboy Industries, the organization in LA run by a friend of hers, Father Gregory Boyle. "He works with gangs," Pema said, "provides them health and social services, teaches them life skills, and helps them get jobs. We were in Father Gregory's office, and a guy came in, frustrated that no one would hire him. Father Boyle suggested that he might have better luck if he removed the tattoo on his forehead that said FUCK LIFE."

When their laughter subsided, Pema turned serious and asked how his practice was going.

"We've talked enlightenment," Jarvis said. "It's been such a trippy idea—too vague for me—but I think I'm getting it more and more."

"What have you discovered?" she asked.

"I sit in the morning and at night," Jarvis said, "but basically I'm meditating all the time now—every minute. I feel like I'm living in a state of meditation. I feel the joy of connecting to my friends on the inside and outside even as I live with the weight of their and others'—everyone's—pain. I'm curious about what's going to happen. I mess up all the time but am grounded every morning when I ask myself questions. They give me peace and power."

She asked, "What are the questions?"

"Back when I first contacted Rinpoche, he sent that old book of his, *Life in Relation to Death*, in which he said people should end their day by asking what they have done with their lives if they died that night. The questions scared the hell out of me then. I'd wasted my life. I'd harmed many people. I have different answers now and ask different questions."

"What are the questions you ask?"

"You once said that karma boils down to the question 'How will I use today?' That's what I ask: How will I use today? Will I be asleep or awake? What will I notice? How can I help? Whose life will I touch?"

They sat in joyful silence until a guard came by to end the visit.

EPILOGUE

LIVING WITH AN OPEN HEART

In the end these things matter most: How well did you love?
How fully did you live? How deeply did you let go?

—Gautama Buddha

My phone chimed at 3:00 a.m., alerting me that a text had arrived. Usually I turn it off at night but I had forgotten, and I looked at the screen. The text came from an unidentified number. It read, "Is this working?"

Then the phone chimed a second time for a second text. This one was a photograph. A selfie.

Dimly lit, sitting in front of a Jimi Hendrix poster, was Jarvis, grinning hugely.

I responded, "WTF."

He wrote back, "What does that mean?"

"What the fuck are you doing with a cell phone?"

It's no surprise that cell phones are banned in San Quentin and other prisons, where telephone access is strictly monitored and controlled. The prohibitions notwithstanding, black-market cell phones are a thriving business in many prisons, including San Quentin. Jarvis bought his phone from an inmate who probably bought it from a guard (Jarvis said it was better not to ask). A friend paid for cell service—and Netflix.

The seller's pitch included the promise of unlimited movies, so Jarvis was disappointed that the cellular signal through the prison walls was insufficient to allow streaming. His phone got only one bar. However, necessity is the mother of invention, and prisoners have a lot of time on their hands, so they often devise ingenious work-arounds. Though the signal was still too weak for streaming, Jarvis learned that he could use some phone apps offline. He could, for instance, take photos, make video and audio recordings, and attach them to texts, which he could then send if he put the phone in a Lay's potato chip bag attached to a wire and slid the package under the cell door and out into the corridor, where the signal was stronger.

A few phone calls got through, and he sent me pictures of his cell and his tier, taken through the mesh that covered the door. He also sent a recording of an inmate complaining that Jarvis's typing was too loud.

As he texted another friend, "[This phone] blew my mind wide open! I mean, 10-12 hours a day! If I had money I could have or-dered a pizza (🍕) [he'd figured out how to use emojis]. Could you see a pizza man at the front gate—'for a Jarvis Masters.'?"

For almost four decades, Jarvis's access to technology was lim-ited to TV, radio, and the electric typewriter Pamela had sent him. When he was arrested at ninteeen, there were no personal comput-ers, never mind internet or smartphones. Once in the 2000s, when he had been in the back of a prison van taking him to the hospital, he delighted in the sights of the blue bay, billowing white clouds, and the golden hills in the distance. When he looked at street cor-ners, he was shocked to see so many people talking to themselves. He remarked on it, and a guard told him they were on the phone, speaking through microphones and listening through earpieces. Other than that, the nearest he'd gotten to modern technology was as it was depicted on TV, where it seemed like science fiction.

Once he learned the potato-chip-bag trick, Jarvis leapfrogged decades forward and could freely communicate with friends when-ever he wanted to and without being spied on. Not only could he send messages, but he could receive them, and friends sent texts, articles, and music videos. I sent him a video I shot while driving across the Golden Gate Bridge, and Jarvis replied that he'd crossed that bridge only in chains.

I also sent a video of a performance by a hip-hop theater com-pany called Truthworker, whose founder and artistic director was his friend Samara Gaev. The performance, written and performed by high-school- and college-aged kids, was based on their correspon-dences and a visit to the prison. Called *IN | PRISM: Boxed In & Blacked*

Out in America, it depicted Jarvis when he was twenty-five, brutalized by guards and accused of murder. The video was a recording of a performance of the play at Lincoln Center in New York City. Jarvis told me he'd watched that video dozens of times, and he cried every time.

A couple of months after Jarvis got the phone, guards conducted a random search and found it; the phone had been hidden inside his copy of the book *We're All Doing Time*.

They also discovered a vape, and Jarvis was written up for the infractions. After a disciplinary hearing, he was sent to solitary, where I visited him. There were no snacks, just the smeared glass wall, like when I first met him more than ten years earlier. It was sad to have a barrier between us again, but Jarvis looked good. As I was thinking that, he looked at me and said, "Man, you look stressed."

I told him I'd gotten a speeding ticket, that my father-in-law fell down and my wife was trying to help him, that we got an astronomical water bill because of a leak, and that I'd spent the morning in bumper-to-bumper traffic, and then, as I pulled off the freeway, some asshole cut me off and flipped me off. I was still frustrated and angry when I looked over at Jarvis and saw that he was smiling. It hit me. "God, I'm sorry," I said. "I'm complaining about *my* life? *Here?*"

Jarvis said, "No, no, no, that's not what I'm thinking. I'm just thinking that you had a hell of a morning. You better relax. You're going to die before me!"

He told me about the only time he'd been in a traffic jam in

his life. He was being driven to the hospital for tests after a seizure, and traffic was at a standstill. The three guards and the driver
were pissed off, but Jarvis was thrilled. He gazed with fascination
at people in their cars. A family was in animated conversation. A
woman was singing. A few drivers were alone, one appeared angry,
and others were stone-faced. He watched them, and his heart
melted.

Decades before, when Jarvis had taken his first Buddhist vows,
Chagdud Tulku Rinpoche gave him a cryptic instruction: he should
learn to see the perfection of all beings. That was what he saw in the
faces of the people in their cars, and he was moved to tears.

Soon after that conversation, I was driving to the airport, and I was
stuck in traffic again. I was feeling angry and stressed, worried that
I'd miss my flight and then I'd miss an event in New York. As I
stewed, traffic crept forward an inch at a time. Suddenly I recalled
Jarvis's traffic jam.

I took a breath, exhaled, and calmed down. Then I looked over
at the car next to mine. The driver was a thin man, old, with wiry
silver hair, unkempt eyebrows, and a lined face. I looked closer and
imagined the full life he'd lived. I guessed he had a partner and possibly children. I knew he'd had much joy and sorrow, as we all do.

I gazed into other cars: a woman on the phone, appearing hard
and angry; another on the phone, solemn; one apparently daydream-
ing; and a man looking ahead with an expression that could have
been annoyance or regret.

I imagined their successes and disappointments.

I was looking through Jarvis's eyes, and I stared at—*into*—people I'd never have noticed. I wasn't in traffic anymore; I was with all those people in a halo of grace somewhere different and better.

I got it then, what Jarvis's first teacher had meant: all those people—in their business and boredom, in their joy and suffering—they *were* perfect.

I visited Jarvis on Christmas Day, 2018, a half year after he'd been released from the AC and gone back to East Block. Because of the crowd of visitors, we met in a different visiting room than usual, filled with thirty or more convicts along with their wives, mothers, children, other family, and friends in cages.

I surveyed the room and noticed a frail woman in her seventies sharing a bag of popcorn with her gray-haired son; a couple holding hands, not talking; a girl of five or six sitting next to her dad, her head resting on his shoulder as he read a Dr. Seuss book to her: *One Fish, Two Fish, Red Fish, Blue Fish*.

I looked into the cages again and thought, *These poor people. These poor children. It's Christmas, come see your father on death row. These poor women. God, what a life.*

Jarvis interrupted my thoughts. "Man," he said, "are you seeing this?" He was scanning the room, too. "Look at these beautiful people. This room is filled with so much love today."

I looked from cage to cage again, and saw what he saw. Where I saw sadness, pain, and regret, Jarvis saw light and joy and love.

POSTSCRIPT

Free your mind and your ass will follow.

—George Clinton, Funkadelic

Two thousand twenty is the thirtieth anniversary of Jarvis's arrival on death row. In August 2019, he had another setback when the California Supreme Court denied his habeas corpus petition. The appeal now moves on to the federal court. He, his attorneys, and his supporters continue to fight to prove his innocence. Meanwhile, Jarvis writes, meditates, celebrates his sangha, and does what he can to help others in prison, whether or not their prison has bars.

ACKNOWLEDGMENTS

I'm grateful to the following friends, supporters, and relatives of Jarvis who shared their stories with me: Patricia Savitri Burbank, Ricky Campbell, Philip Coffin, Carol Dodson, Sherri Forester, Samara Gaev, Chris Grosso, Kelly Hayden, Barbara Jacobsen, Cliff Johnson, Janis Kobe, Corny Koehl, Parker Krasney, Lee Lesser, Harline Masters, Michele Modena, Susan Moon, Sara Paris, Connie Pham, Samantha Sanderson, Jan Sells, Will Shonbrun, Blaise Smith, Freddie Taylor, and Mark Werlin. I'm also indebted to Jarvis's attorneys: Joe Baxter, Scott Kauffman, Michael Satris, and Rick Targow; and researchers Mariel Brunman, Phoebe Bryan, and Josh Stadtner.

Special thanks to Ernest Rogers, legal visiting coordinator at

San Quentin, who was endlessly patient, accommodating, and kind during my many visits to death row.

I particularly want to acknowledge the contributions of Melody Ermachild, Marty Krasney, Glenna Olmsted, Alan Senauke, Susan Shannon, Raven, Lama Shenpen, and Rebecca Solnit, all of whom offered their invaluable support and insight.

And then there's Jarvis's friend, teacher, and "mom," Pema Chödrön. Ani Pema has inspired countless people around the world and helped them to face the challenges in their lives. She has certainly inspired and helped me—with this book and in my own life. Her devotion to Jarvis is moving beyond words.

At ICM, I'm eternally grateful to my agent, Amanda Urban. I've been immensely lucky to have worked with Binky for—it's hard to fathom—thirty-five years. I'm thankful for her guidance, wisdom, and friendship.

At Simon & Schuster, I wish to thank Tzipora Baitch, Nicole Hines, Sara Kitchen, Ruth Lee-Mui, Zoe Norvell, Julia Prosser, Brianna Scharfenberg, and others on the S&S team who supported this book.

My deepest thanks to my editor, Eamon Dolan. I can never fully express my gratitude and affection for Eamon—the way he has helped me express myself in my books. *The Buddhist on Death Row* simply would not exist without him. He envisioned the book, understood it, and believed in it—and, against all reason, in me—even when I was lost, discouraged, and two years past my deadline. Eamon's vision, wisdom, and sublime editing are present on every page. As editor, he's unparalleled. As friend, he's one in a billion. Those lucky enough to know him understand when I say that

Eamon is a true bodhisattva—endlessly compassionate, devoted to alleviating suffering and creating a more just world.

It's impossible to adequately express my gratitude to Jarvis Masters. It's been a hell of a ride together marked by tears and laughter. Thanks to Jarvis for his trust and friendship, which I cherish.

Finally, to my children, Daisy, Jasper, and Nic Sheff, and my wife, Karen Barbour—as Ray Davies (for whom I'm also grateful) says: You make it all worthwhile.

ONE PLACE. MANY STORIES

Bold, innovative and
empowering publishing.

FOLLOW US ON:

@HQStories